Praise for *Freedom Is an Inside Job*

"Not often does a book hold up a mirror to our souls, helping us to find courage and inspiration from within. Here Salbi gives us an extraordinary personal story, told with touching candidness that, though unique to her life, will deeply resonate with women all across the world. Her human approach to hard issues is shaped by compassion, intelligence, and emotional wisdom. Deeply human, sensitive, and sturdy, Salbi's writing will heal hearts."

ELIF ŞAFAK
author of the bestselling *The Bastard of Istanbul*,
The Forty Rules of Love, and *Three Daughters of Eve*

"If you want to know what true self-power is, then read this book. Zainab Salbi, a modern-day icon of empowerment and an inspiration to millions of women and to men like myself, shares her journey from an environment of subjugation and cruel circumstances to inner freedom and leadership. The poet Rumi said, 'Why do you stay in prison when the door is wide open?' The prison is the mind-forged shackles of our own conditioning. Zainab's book will open your inner eye to the beauty of your own being."

DEEPAK CHOPRA, MD
author of *The Healing Self* and
The Seven Spiritual Laws of Success

"A true spiritual seeker must eventually search inside her own self. This Zainab Salbi does with great consistency and courage in *Freedom Is an Inside Job*. Sharing her discoveries with determination and resolve, she demonstrates what is possible for anyone who sincerely desires to be part of a new imagination for changing the world."

ALICE WALKER
author of *The Color Purple* and
The World Will Follow Joy

"Freedom comes from telling our own story, and empathy comes from listening to the stories of people very different from us. Zainab Salbi inspires us to do both. May her book help create bridges to a much bigger and kinder world."

GLORIA STEINEM
author of *My Life on the Road* and *Revolution from Within*

"What Zainab Salbi has given us with this book is a tremendous act of courage. *Freedom Is an Inside Job* is a deeply felt revelation of Zainab's heart and mind and her hopes for a better world. She provides for us all an example of what searching within ourselves can look like, and the powerful results of such a journey. We owe her no less than our thanks, but also to follow her exacting lead."

MYCHAL DENZEL SMITH
New York Times bestselling author of
Invisible Man, Got the Whole World Watching

"In this prescient and timely work, Salbi offers us a path to personal authenticity and freedom. It is an inner journey that demands we see with absolute clarity both the light and darkness we harbor within."

SHARON SALZBERG
cofounder of Insight Meditation Society
and author of *Real Love*

"Zainab Salbi has written exactly the book we need for our fear-ridden and divided world. It's time for each of us to do our own work and embody the change we want to see; only then, from a place of fullness, can we light the way ahead. Read this book and then help point the way for others."

ARIANNA HUFFINGTON
founder of Huffington Post and
author of *On Becoming Fearless* and *Thrive*

"There could not be a more critical time to read this book—and act as it recommends—than now, in these incredibly divisive times. In beautiful prose, and with extraordinarily moving stories, Zainab Salbi shows us how we can open ourselves to ourselves—and then to others—and actually then reach across seemingly impossible divides to achieve healing for the human condition. All of us who seek justice—and anybody who seeks understanding—must start here, with compassion. This book is like a salve for our collective wounds—we all need it now."

SARU JAYARAMAN
attorney, activist, and author of *Forked*

"*Freedom Is an Inside Job* is a remarkable testament to the adage that only what we achieve inwardly can change outer reality. Zainab Salbi's courageously honest journey to excavate her innermost truths and reveal her truest self is a precious gift for anyone who aspires to live their fullest and truest life. It's equally an essential guide for leaders devoted to making the lives of others better. Readers who join Zainab on her quest for true freedom will be inspired to emulate her humble and bold example."

DOV SEIDMAN
bestselling author of *How: Why How
We Do Anything Means Everything*

Freedom
is an inside job

Also by Zainab Salbi

Between Two Worlds: Escape from Tyranny:
Growing Up in the Shadow of Saddam (with Laurie Becklund)

The Other Side of War: Women's Stories of Survival and Hope

If You Knew Me You Would Care
(with photographs by Rennio Maifredi)

ZAINAB SALBI

Freedom
is an inside job

OWNING OUR DARKNESS AND OUR LIGHT
TO HEAL OURSELVES AND THE WORLD

sounds true
BOULDER, COLORADO

Sounds True
Boulder, CO 80306

Some names and identifying details have been changed
to protect the privacy of individuals.

Published 2018

Cover design by Jennifer Miles
Book design by Beth Skelley
Cover image © Nick Hernandez

Printed in Canada

Library of Congress Cataloging-in-Publication Data

Names: Salbi, Zainab, author.
Title: Freedom is an inside job : owning our darkness and our light to heal
    ourselves and the world / Zainab Salbi.
Description: Boulder, Colorado : Sounds True, 2018.
Identifiers: LCCN 2018010358 (print) | LCCN 2018027962 (ebook) |
    ISBN 9781683642060 (ebook) | ISBN 9781683641773 (hardcover)
Subjects: LCSH: Self-actualization (Psychology) | Social change.
Classification: LCC BF637.S4 (ebook) | LCC BF637.S4 S2344 2018 (print) |
    DDC 158.1—dc23
LC record available at https://lccn.loc.gov/2018010358

10 9 8 7 6 5 4 3 2 1

To my Baba, my teacher in love,
and
A. B., my teacher in life.

Contents

The Girl Who Sings

Once upon a time, a girl in a green dress lay forgotten at the bottom of a ship. Her hands and feet were tied, and she lay among hundreds of slaves, one next to the other. They had been in captivity for a long, long time, and in the shadowy bottom of the boat, it was not clear if they were dead or alive. Dust covered their bodies.

One day, a mouse started gnawing on the girl's ropes, and she woke up. As she stretched and looked around, the ropes that had bound her for so long frayed and broke. With that she was able to stand up.

Liberated, she looked at the others around her and saw that they had all died in their sleep. Afraid and alone, she stood in the darkness of the bottom of the ship, thick with the smell of death. She began to sing softly. The melody had no words, but it made a unique sound—the sound of her life. As the tune took shape and her voice strengthened, she felt less scared and alone. Her body magically rose up and up and up until she entered another reality.

In this new world, the girl found herself on a bustling city street where people were rushing from one place to the other. Cars were speeding by and honking. She didn't recognize anyone or anything. All she knew how to do was to keep on singing the song of her life.

Her voice was so beautiful that passersby stopped to listen. As more people noticed her singing, they talked about her, and she became popular. People were whistling her melodies and seeking her out wherever she'd wandered in the city. Since no one knew who she was, they called her the Girl Who Sings. She became more and more known. More and more people wanted to hear her.

One day, people got together and built a clay statue to put her inside so they could hear her whenever they wanted. At first she went along with their plan, but soon she realized that being in the statue was like being tied with ropes at the bottom of the ship. Both were forms of enslavement. She was not trying to please anybody; she was simply singing the sound of her heart. That is what made her sound so moving. To stay inside the dark statue was to suffocate.

So she decided to break free. Singing and singing the song of her life, she was lifted again into another reality, one very different from the bustling city.

In this third level of reality, she found a woman wearing a black robe, a black headdress, and a black mask. The woman was stirring a bubbling stew in a large cauldron over a fire. The girl walked toward the black pot. As she got closer, the woman spoke.

"You must accept evil," she said mysteriously.

Scared, the Girl Who Sings retreated. She could not accept evil. It was too much to ask. When she retreated, the woman stopped stirring the stew. But the girl was still curious, so she walked forward again.

The woman in the black mask repeated, "You must accept evil."

The girl stepped back again, afraid. She could not accept evil. But every time she took a step back, the woman in the black mask stopped stirring the stew. Everything paused.

The girl realized that whatever the woman was trying to make could not continue unless she accepted evil. Eventually, her curiosity took over. She wanted to know what would happen if the cooking continued. She approached the cauldron again, and when asked for the third time to accept evil, she agreed. Immediately, a ceremony began. The stew began to bubble and boil, and the woman began stirring more intensely. The woman spoke. "Now you must choose one of these white masks hanging on the wall behind you."

The girl looked at the wall of masks. She did not like any of them. She turned to the woman and pointed at her face and said, "I want your mask."

"No one has ever asked me for my mask before," said the woman, perplexed. "But here, wear it."

As soon as the Girl Who Sings donned the black mask, Evil arrived. It was neither a man nor a woman. It was a faceless being in a charcoal robe. Evil held out its charcoal-gloved hand for the girl to take. She did so hesitantly, and they walked away, leaving the woman behind.

Evil and the girl walked and walked until they arrived at Evil's land. It was a vast, dark field crowded with people. Some were lying down, and others were standing. All were covered in spider webs. The girl's eyes opened wide; it was a horrifying scene. These people had surrendered to living this way, stuck forever in the land of Evil.

"You see all these people—they are in this field because of something they did that they are ashamed of," Evil said. "Some stole, some lied, and some did something sexual. Their shame is what brings them here.

"What they don't know is that they have a choice," Evil continued. "I am not keeping them here by force. Not at all. They each can walk away from here. All they need to do is to acknowledge what they did and talk about it. Then, they can leave. Anyone can do it. But when their shame and fear are stronger than their strength to do their work, they don't make this choice. They don't free themselves."

The girl realized that the reason she had to accept evil was to see this field. She needed to understand why people stayed stuck in Evil's land. *It is shame and fear that keep us wrapped in these sticky spider webs,* she thought. *It is not Evil itself.*

Evil wanted to show her something else, so they continued walking. They went into a building, through one giant door after another, from one room to another. At last they entered a small room with a chest in the middle. Evil opened the chest and unlocked a box inside it. In that box was another, smaller box. Evil opened that one and kept going until it reached the smallest box. Evil carefully opened it. It contained a heart. It was Evil's heart that had been hidden for a very long time. Evil was showing it to her alone.

"Only someone who sings the true song of her life can hold this heart," Evil said. Evil offered its heart to her. "Please take it with you. You are free to leave this land."

The girl looked at the heart and saw that it was just a normal beating heart, neither good nor bad. She took the heart and swallowed it. Now, she had courage.

To leave the land of Evil, the Girl Who Sings had to cross a rope bridge and walk through a murky forest alone. The bridge was made of half-broken wooden planks and loose ropes that barely held together. The dark forest that loomed on the other side seemed mysterious and ominous. The Girl Who Sings was paralyzed with fear. She did not know what to do.

Suddenly, she remembered what had helped her leave the bottom of the ship—the song of her life. She began to sing with all her heart, and as she became absorbed in the sound again, she grew happy. Her melodies and her voice brought her joy, and that joy gave her the strength to cross the bridge. It helped her go through the dark forest without fear. She just kept on singing. She remembered that it was her choice to see her fear and her shame. It was her choice to be free. Her happiness relieved her worries and gave her more courage.

The girl sang until she was lifted up to a final layer of reality. There she found herself in a field of light blue. All the people there were moving freely, dancing with happiness. They laughed, sang, played, talked, and expressed themselves openly without worry or fear. The girl smiled. As she took a step forward to enter the land of freedom, she realized that this would be the first time that Evil's heart—the heart she had swallowed—would experience beauty, joy, and freedom after being locked up in a box for what might have been eternity.

With that realization, she stepped into her own freedom.

Introduction

We are living in a time of shadows. What is ugly in our world is rising out of the basement where we have locked it up for a long time. Countries, communities, and individuals are divided into extremes: left and right, rich and poor, citizen and foreigner, Muslim and Christian, ruler and rebel, employer and employee, man and woman, all of us with vastly different points of view that seem never to agree. This is creating panic and confusion.

As an Iraqi-born Muslim American who has worked most of her life in service to victims of war, especially women, I have lived through instability and unrest, have known dictators and world leaders, have dodged snipers' bullets and fought for justice. I have tried to address some of the world's rights and wrongs through my humanitarian work in war zones and later in my media projects that shared some of the struggles and triumphs of people around the world, from the third-gender movement in India to the wives of ISIS in Iraq to young Muslim Americans deciding to wear the head scarf. I know conflict, struggle, and division intimately. And I have learned that when we lead with fear and anger, we eventually become the very aggressors we are fighting against. We become what we despise.

This is especially important to understand right now. All over the world, we are pointing our fingers in fear and anger at perceived enemies and aggressors around us. Afraid and bewildered, we are searching for the "other" to confront. As someone who travels between the two worlds of the West and the East, the United States and the Middle East, I see the different fingers pointing. Whenever I am in the Middle East, I hear that everything is America's fault.

All the destruction, revolutions, oppressions—even ISIS—stem from America's arrogance and abuse of power. Ironically, I hear the same from the other direction: to Americans, all this terrorism, instability, fear, and mass displacement of people is because of the depravity and corruption of those "other" people *over there*, in those Godforsaken places far away.

Indeed, there are plenty of people we could point fingers at. We can point at the people who voted for Trump or Brexit or in the referendums in Catalonia or Kurdistan. We can point at the mass migration from Syria or the destabilizing force of Russia. Or we can point our fingers closer to home, at people who practice different religious customs than we do, at bosses who block our progress, or at family members who abuse us.

We could—but this is not a book of how we got here or who is to blame. This book is about "Now what?" Now that we see ourselves pointing our fingers in accusation at one another, what do we do about this turmoil?

Each life, each place, each culture, each individual has the good, the bad, and the ugly within it. We all have a story, and it's usually complex. When we demonize or idealize *anyone*, we remove ourselves from the picture and oversimplify the situation. We do it when we think all Afghan men are oppressive and all Canadians are peacemakers or when we say all conservatives are closed-minded and cruel whereas all liberals are open-minded and compassionate. We do it when we think all male bosses are bullies and all female bosses are role models. These generalizations may be convenient, and some may contain a grain of truth, but they cannot be fully true. When we demonize or idealize, we lose any sense that we *also* carry the good, the bad, and the ugly in us as well. We lose sight of the fact that we all have a story. And from our stories we all make choices.

We need to find another way to deal with our panic and confusion. Now is the time. We need not only to talk about what is wrong with our world but also to find a *way* to talk to one another and cross the divides. In the West, many of us want to be the hero of our own movie. We want to see ourselves on the side of the good, speaking truth to power like Wonder Woman or Spider-Man. It's a noble inclination, but we don't always see the whole picture. We don't understand what's at stake for the other side. And we certainly don't understand our role in it. What have we done ourselves, as good people, as innocent, caring people, to encourage this troubling division and turmoil?

We need a new way to think about this broken time. We need a new language in order to connect with those we consider "other," different from us, and whose actions we find hard to comprehend. We need to harness our desire to do good and put it to its best use. Because unless we know what it means to be a hero in all the small ways of our lives—in our marriages and families, in our work and social lives, and in how we account for our past actions and current values—we will not become that hero we fantasize about. If we talk only about the big stories and big traumas out there, we can easily hide from our own stories and our own shadows inside ourselves. Our reactivity and self-righteousness will create more division, turmoil, anger, and hatred. Then, *we* become the polarizing force. As we stab our fingers at "the enemy," we ourselves create enemies.

True change starts with owning our own experiences. That means owning the good and the bad and the ugly in ourselves—as well as what makes us beautiful. It means owning the complexity of our emotions and dreams, as well as the discomfort of our missteps and misfortunes. It means being deliberate and aware of our actions. Then we are not intellectualizing our lives. We are not operating from the narrow simplicity of merely *thinking* about things or *reacting* to them. Then, we are talking from the depths of our known selves. We stand on the wisdom of our lived experiences. We are no longer available to being manipulated by others who want to tap into the shadows that we carry but cannot bear to face.

It is scary, at times, to share what I and others have grappled with, but it is the only way I know to be authentic to myself, to you, and to the world we are living in. It's a journey inward, a journey of the brave, a journey of transformation. I won't lie: it is indeed a bumpy road. But it's very much worth traveling for the ultimate freedom we gain personally and for what we contribute to the well-being of the collective.

It is with this spirit that I share my own stories and experiences in this book, as well as the stories and experiences of many others who are also coming face-to-face with their core truths. By sharing these stories openly, I hope to illuminate this path for those who also feel called to connect with their own. We cannot talk about any value outwardly if we do not understand it inwardly first.

I began to wake up to what is good, bad, and ugly within myself when I decided to write my memoir, *Between Two Worlds: Escape from Tyranny: Growing Up in the Shadow of Saddam*, which was published in 2006, and reveal truths that had been too painful to admit for most of my adult life. As I awakened and began to sing the song of my life, I also had to reckon with what was broken in myself. I hadn't wanted to face the dreams, the ideals, the behaviors, and the attitudes that had not worked, nor the situations that had been beyond my control. Writing that memoir was not easy, as I talk about in chapter 1, but it was essential. The taste of freedom that came from it was so delicious that it inspired me to examine my whole life this way.

This awakening led me to unravel all the other layers of untruth in my life. It didn't happen overnight, and it was also painful at times, as you'll read: it was hard to leave my gentle and loving husband when our marriage faltered; it was hard to step down from Women for Women International, the organization I had founded and that, for twenty years, had helped hundreds of thousands of women around the world; and it was hard to face the shame of understanding that I, too, could be arrogant. At first, seeing my inner "other" horrified and depressed me. It took time to realize that it was an important wake-up call.

In the process of exposing my secrets and fear by writing my memoir, I discovered that I could trust in the process of unwinding the layers of my truth. That trust led me down paths I hadn't realized were open to me. I discovered what it meant to be truly happy. I realized my own beauty—and that it had been there all along. I confronted my terror and found that I could have compassion even for the one who terrified me. I, who had always identified as a fighter, learned the beauty and power of surrender.

If we do not take the time to get quiet, go inward, acknowledge what has happened, and see who we are in all of our goodness and ugliness, we act out. When we do not sing the songs of our lives, we become angry, self-righteous, cruel, or even violent. That's when we lose ourselves in twisted half-truths or outright lies.

On my inward journey, I saw that we all need to dig deeper to speak and live according to our real values, not the ones we think we are supposed to have. We need to see our shadows and know our darknesses. We need to understand a deeper dimension of our truths, one beyond finger-pointing. Only then can we really speak and act in alignment. Then, we can look at what is dark in our world right now and ask, honestly, without an agenda, "Why is this happening?" Once our own dark and light are more integrated, our voices of protest change from harsh barks that speak to some but alienate others to a resonant call that many, many more people can hear.

Awakening creates a bridge to our authenticity. With that comes a more honest conversation inside ourselves and with others. We can see our shadows and our light, our demons and our beauty. We can speak about the larger issues with credibility and integrity. When we wake up, we can have a more honest way of relating to those closest to us and also to those whose lives we've never given any thought to. That's when we can begin to better understand the world around us. Only when I began to see that "other" within myself could I truly see the "other" in them, in the "rednecks" of America, the "Arabs" of France, the "fundamentalists" of Islam—and in all of us. From there, we start to bridge the divide between us and them, between the many "others" out there and our inner "other" whom we live with every day.

A true hero is an ordinary person who can hold the sword of truth and tell the full truth of herself, in her good, her bad, and her ugly qualities. She makes her choices from this understanding. As heroes, we move forward, not in fear and anger, but in integrity, love, and vision. We work from the strength of our spines rather than the breathlessness of our chests.

If we have the courage to look inward and embrace truth in our lives—the entire truth—then we may gain the courage and the credibility to look outward and become a force of great change in this world. We will see our own role in the world we have created. Then we will charge forward *for* something, not simply *against* something. And from our collective integrity and values, the change we are seeking will necessarily happen.

We have all the tools we need to begin. It's simple, really, because all we need is ourselves.

It begins with us.

1

Telling Our Stories

Only when we tell our stories
can there be real healing.

For the longest time, the dynamic of "us" versus "them" was just how I saw the world. I thought in terms of good and bad, just and unjust, freedom and oppression. I thought of the Americans around me in my adopted country of the United States as free and courageous, while Iraqis back home were oppressed and victimized. America was the land of liberty, whereas Iraq, where I was born and grew up, was as suffocating as a prison.

As I lived more of my life in America and less in Iraq, and as I worked in more and more war-ravaged countries around the world, I slowly came to realize that the good, the bad, and the ugly exist everywhere. Harm and pain did not come only from an authoritarian dictator or an abusive husband; they also came through words and actions of self-proclaimed enlightened Americans who saw themselves as spiritual, open-minded, and committed to personal growth. Seeing that there were no utopias in this world after all was like falling out of heaven.

The problem lay in how I romanticized the concept of "us" and demonized the concept of "them." I thought one culture and one way of life was superior to another. I was wrong. That realization opened up the doors to more realizations. *Maybe* I had hurt people even though I identified very strongly as someone who *helped* others, not betrayed them. My life had embodied the values of a selfless activist who worked with the poor and with victims of war. Everything I did was for them. But I started to see that what I had deemed *good* wasn't perfect after all—including myself. I wasn't exempt from the bad. I, too, had a shadow.

We all have a story, no matter who we are or where we come from. The story of our lives tells of our goodness and our suffering, our privilege and our complicity, our light and our shadow, and much more. It has its own particular melody and harmony, rhythm and cadence. Most of us hide the full story of our lives and tell only the good part. I know I did!

It wasn't until I met Nabintu, a Congolese woman in her early fifties, that I realized that I had a story to share with the wider world. I thought I was helping *her* after her life had been shattered in a vicious militia attack. In reality, she gave me a piece of wisdom that changed my life.

I met Nabintu in 2003 in the Democratic Republic of Congo when I was thirty-four years old and had been working with victims of war for more than a decade. It was an early visit to DR Congo to see if we could expand the humanitarian work of Women for Women International, the organization I had founded in the United States in 1993. As well as offering immediate financial aid to women survivors of war, I always made sure to listen to women's stories. Women needed to be heard. I also wanted to be able share these stories with those who were involved with our organization. Knowing the dire realities that women like Nabintu faced helped to raise support for women survivors of wars everywhere. Over time, we would also try to offer these women education and vocational training.

By the time I met Nabintu, I'd heard thousands of stories like hers, stories from women incarcerated in rape camps in Bosnia, caught in the genocide in Rwanda, or denied education and other basic rights by the Taliban in Afghanistan. I'd heard countless stories of women doing everything they could to keep their families alive, fed, and together. Too often, war relief ignores the traumas that women in war suffer; we wanted to find ways to support her as we had so many other women.

Nabintu's story was horrifying but not unique. It started when a faction of violent rebels descended on her village. When she saw them coming, she hid under her bed, but the rebels found her anyway, as well as her three daughters, aged nine, twenty-one, and twenty-two. The men forced them to the ground, spreading open their arms and legs, circling in a wild urge to take their turn. They raped them all. There were so many men around her daughters that Nabintu lost count. They ordered Nabintu's son to spread his mother's legs as they raped her. Then, they commanded him to rape his own mother. When he refused, they shot him in the foot.

The rebels' violence did not stop there. They ransacked Nabintu's home, pillaging what they wanted and burning everything else—the house, the clothes, every dish and stick of furniture. Nabintu and her daughters were left naked. Neighbors who had survived the rebel attacks came quickly and lent them each a piece of cloth to use as a dress. When I met Nabintu shortly after, she had moved from her village, fearing another attack. She was wearing that same dress that her neighbors had given her on that terrible day. It was the only one she owned. She'd made shoes from material she plucked from piles of garbage in her new neighborhood.

For all the atrocities I have seen over so many years, I never stop being shocked at the cruelty of humanity. Although I always tried to control my tears in front of the women I was interviewing, my tears never dried up. I would worry if they did.

As she finished telling her story, Nabintu looked me in the eyes. "I have never told this story to anybody else but you."

I took a deep breath. "Nabintu, I am a storyteller. I share stories like yours throughout the world to raise support and attention to what is happening to women in war-torn places like DR Congo. Should I keep your story a secret?" I needed to be honest with her. The support I would raise in using her story would not all go to her. Some of it would, and the rest would help many other women like her.

She smiled. "If I could tell the whole world about my story, I would, so that other women would not have to go through what I have gone through. But I can't. You can. You go ahead and tell the world, just not to my new neighbors."

Every now and then, we hear a piece of wisdom that hits us like an arrow straight to the center of our hearts. This was one of these moments for me. Nabintu was illiterate, poor, homeless, and a victim of horrific violence. Yet she had a profound clarity about the connection between one woman's story and the larger collective of women's stories. She knew if one woman broke her silence, she might help to spare other women from what she herself had suffered. If the world knew, it could intervene and stop the atrocities that led to millions of people killed and hundreds of thousands of women and girls raped.

I hugged Nabintu and promised to tell her story. I talked to my staff about getting Nabintu immediate help to start rebuilding her life. Then, I left. I had a five-hour drive ahead of me, over the nearby border to Kigali, the capital of Rwanda, for more meetings and more interviews. As I got in the car, I started to cry. My tears were not only for Nabintu and what she had gone through; they were also an expression of my own shame.

Nabintu had the courage I did not have. She had lost everything, but she still had her voice, and she wanted to use it. Not me. I hid my own story and pretended not to have one. My job was to get *other* women to break their silence and to share their stories. I never wanted to risk sharing my own. For the longest time I told myself, *I have no story to tell.*

Like many educated, liberal, activist women, I was passionate about the plight of other women whom I considered more disadvantaged than myself. I had grown up in an upper-middle-class family, had traveled around the world, gone to school and university, enjoyed relative safety and security. In my mind, whatever I or my family had gone through in Iraq, even as Saddam Hussein rose to power, was not as severe or extreme as what these women had gone through—these women who were not only poor but had survived unthinkable violence. My material privilege provided an easy cover: *someone like me did not have a story.* But underneath that cover, I was embarrassed to share the fullness of my experience. How could I be a strong women's rights activist when I had been in an arranged marriage, had been raped, and had suffered from all the fears and uncertainties of growing up in a dictatorship?

Either from ignorance or self-righteousness, I preached empowerment as if I had mastered my own power as a woman. But I hadn't. I was asking women like Nabintu to do something that I was not willing to do myself. I was asking them to tell the whole world about what had happened to them, in spite of their fears of being judged or ostracized by their families and communities and the real risks that went along with that. But I was not willing to do the same. I could not comprehend the risks they were taking in any personal way.

The truth is, in hiding what I'd lived through and thinking that it was not a big deal, I was creating a differentiation of "us" and "them" that allowed me to stay separate from the very women I was serving. Like many well-intentioned humanitarians, I was unconsciously acting as the savior. By default, this made the women I was working with into helpless victims who needed saving. This position gave me no claim to suffering, while allowing these women no claim to wisdom. I was seeing the world through two separate paradigms that would never require me to stand in my truth.

When at last I checked into my hotel in Kigali, Rwanda, I was exhausted from so much thinking and crying, but I was clearheaded. I knew I had two choices: to keep my silence and leave my humanitarian work, or to break my silence and continue on with Women for Women International. It was not a simple choice. To tell my story meant breaking the code of silence I had been trained to keep all my life both as a woman and as a member of a family that had known Saddam Hussein. It meant putting out my dirty laundry for all to see and risking my family's safety and reputation. There was also all the suppressed pain, fear, and shame to process.

Still, I couldn't continue to do my work with women authentically if I stayed silent. I decided to write a memoir to tell the whole world my story. I did not want to hide anymore. It was not easy. In fact, it was a journey of fear and a walk of humility. I held onto the wisdom shared by Nabintu that if I spoke my truth, other women might feel less alone, and that they, too, would find their own paths to freedom no matter what they had suffered. I did not know how hard it would be to break my silence. But I also didn't know how very worthwhile it would be either.

∗

My name is Zainab Salbi. I was my parents' firstborn in Baghdad, Iraq, a child they credited for bringing them luck as they built our family home a year after my birth.

That family home, a two-story, middle-class house in the Al Mansour neighborhood, was nestled in a grove of eucalyptus trees at the end of a quiet cul-de-sac. It witnessed the happy early years of my childhood. As the family of a commercial pilot, we traveled a lot. My mother, a teacher, loved beautiful things, so our home was full of furniture, paintings, and carpets from all over the world. She loved new sets of silver utensils or patterned china. I remember how excited she was about our dining table from Thailand, one with detailed engravings of villages, mountains, and rivers.

While my mother decorated the home, my father tended the garden, nurturing gardenias, roses, and many fruit trees, like fig, pear, and orange. It was if the garden were his second daughter. Little did I know that one day this would all be gone.

Our family home became a symbol of the fate of Iraq itself. In 1973, my parents met Saddam Hussein, then the vice president of Iraq. In a carefully calculated move, he surprised a group of young urban couples, including my parents, who were having a boat party at the Tigris River. All of their lives changed that day. Each couple inevitably had to decide whether to accept Saddam's friendship or refuse it, knowing that either decision would change their lives forever. To refuse was to risk their own lives and the lives of everyone in their extended families. My parents accepted the friendship. They kept it from me and my younger brothers until, one afternoon after he became president, Saddam openly visited our home. Thus, he declared his friendship publicly, not only to our family and neighbors but to the entire country. Our association with him was sealed.

Soon after, Saddam Hussein appointed my father his private commercial pilot and the head of Iraqi civil aviation. Life formally changed after that. We became the family of Saddam Hussein's pilot, living in the house of Saddam Hussein's pilot and in the streets that led to Saddam Hussein's pilot. Our home was monitored, our social life limited to our relationship with Saddam in the surroundings he chose. We children were enlisted in this friendship and all its outings. My teenage years and the childhoods of my two younger brothers were very restricted. We had to behave perfectly, never speak of our family's relationship publicly, and always laugh when Saddam laughed and cry when he cried.

Our lives revolved around the friendship with him. Like all of the other families around him, we lived in constant fear, yet we hid it behind plastic smiles, pretending that we were freely enjoying our relationship with him, that we had no opinions, that no matter what violence he perpetrated—such as killing thousands of Kurds in a poison-gas attack or bulldozing entire Shia communities to settle a political score—he was always right. My family had no political ambition and thus was not a threat to Saddam. Our role was to entertain him and talk about all aspects of urbane contemporary life, from food to fashion to music. We were the jesters of his palace.

I knew life had changed before I understood the reasons. The garden where my parents had parties throughout the seventies was silent in the eighties. Instead of my mother's loud laughter, the garden filled with her tears. She'd pull plastic chairs into the middle of the yard under my father's persimmon tree, turn the radio up loud, and mumble secrets to her friends as she silently wept. It would be a very long time before I understood why.

Throughout this time, my mother would make me read books meant to foster my independence, as a person and as a woman. I read Alex Haley's *Roots: The Saga of an American Family*, as well as feminist books in Arabic, such as one called *I Am Free*. My mother would shake me and say, "Never let anybody abuse you. Never let anybody talk to you or touch you in the wrong way. Always be strong. Always be independent. And never cry."

As a teenager, I could not understand why she was so adamant about these things. But I understood that I needed to be strong. When I declared to her at fifteen that I was going to dedicate myself to helping women, she said, "And you can, honey."

Her insistence on my strength and independence made sense only after I found myself stranded in America. When I was a nineteen-year-old college student in Baghdad, my mother begged me to accept a marriage proposal from a man we had met once on a trip to the United States. It was perplexing. Why would she, who had insisted that I make my own choices and marry for love, ask me to marry a total stranger? That's what more conservative Iraqi families did, not ours. I felt betrayed. But she cried so much, I knew I couldn't disappoint her. My father begged her not to let it happen. "It is just wrong!" he said, over and over. "Do not let your mother's emotion sway you!" But my mother just cried more. So I accepted, even though my father, my brothers, and even my mother were crying every step of the way as we all traveled to the United States to attend my wedding. I did not understand why this was happening, but I wanted to be a good daughter. When my mother whispered, "I don't care what you do while you are in America. Just leave, just leave," I went.

The wedding happened. An arranged marriage does not mean a forced marriage. The choice was ultimately mine. I chose to marry the stranger in order to stop my mother from crying.

Yet the marriage was a horrible one. My husband was an Iraqi American whose family had fled Iraq a decade earlier, when Saddam had come to power. He was thirteen years older than me, very cold and controlling. Because he and his family hated Saddam, he also seemed to hate me, as if I were a proxy for the dictator. Everyone, even ex-pat Iraqis, knew who my father was to the dictator.

At first, my husband agreed that I could continue my college education and handle my own money. But once the marriage documents were signed and my family had returned to Iraq, his attitude changed as I was left in the United States with him. He did everything my mother had told me not to accept. He ordered me to cook, clean, and get on with the business of producing children. He gave me a tiny allowance of twenty dollars a week. He would allow me to take college classes only once my household duties were done, essentially making it impossible to finish my degree. But worse than any of that, he was forceful, vindictive, and cruel during sex.

I asked my mother-in-law to appeal to my husband. Couldn't he treat me more gently? She only rebuked me: "It is your wifely duty to satisfy my son's needs!"

Then, Saddam invaded Kuwait. Iraq was immediately placed under heavy sanctions. A month after my wedding, all phone lines and borders were cut off, and I could not contact my family at all. There was no chance now that I could go back.

The turning point came just three months into the marriage. It was shortly after my twenty-first birthday. I had been trying to be a "good" wife until then, but the conditions felt like enslavement, and I didn't want to pretend anymore. So when I disagreed with my husband over some small matter, we fought, and later that day I refused to have sex with him. Furious, he threw me on the bed and raped me, forcing my head down into the pillow as if to suffocate me.

I sat in the shower for a long time afterward, trembling, hurt, and scared. I had no country, no family, and no plan of what to do next. But I was also angry. I had managed to save four hundred dollars in cash, and I had two suitcases of designer clothes and fancy jewelry from my family. I vowed to get out. And so I fled.

Angels appeared out of nowhere to help me. An old friend of my mother's picked me up and let me stay with her. Over the next six months, an uncle of my father whom I had barely met before asked me to move in with him until I could stand on my feet in this country. The officer at the Immigration and Naturalization Service, as it was called back then, gave me a work permit I had no idea I was eligible for. An Italian American family gave me a job at their Hallmark store. With my initial paycheck, I filed for divorce and bought myself a car, getting my first taste of freedom as an adult.

I could have gone back to Iraq when the Persian Gulf War ended, a few months after I left my husband, but I decided to stay in America. My country was now destroyed. I vowed that I would return one day to help, but before that I wanted to build my life here. I had been given a chance at freedom, and I didn't want to pass it up, no matter how badly I missed my family and the way of life I knew.

My decision meant that I was not able to see my father and two brothers for nine long years. Saddam Hussein was still in power, manipulating the lives of the Iraqi people. The United Nations' sanctions were hurting Iraqis far more than they were hurting Iraq's leaders. Travel, communications, and basic necessities like food, clean water, electricity, and medicine were severely restricted. I heard my family's voices on two-minute phone calls each week—the only time Saddam allowed for any international call. Plus my mother had fled to Jordan, taking one of my brothers with her. This angered Saddam, and in punishment my father was forced to resign from his job. Our family was not killed, but they were socially, economically, and politically ostracized, making life much more difficult.

In contrast, my life in the United States began to flourish. I met a man, fell in love, and chose to marry for a second time. This time, it was a great match. My husband was very kind and intelligent and very gentle with me. He was an activist from a Palestinian American family and was doing his doctorate at the University of Virginia. I also went back to school, this time at George Mason University, to finish my undergraduate education. In college, I started learning about the Holocaust and how people had said, "Never again"—humanity would never again allow atrocities such as genocide to happen. Yet at that very moment in 1993 we were seeing images from Bosnia and Herzegovina of concentration camps—and, as I learned, of rape camps where women were captured by Serbian soldiers to use as sex slaves for months at a time. I was twenty-three years old, a newlywed with no money and no experience. But I felt that I had the responsibility to do something about injustice now that I was living in America. I was free to act without fear. Together with my new husband, Amjad, we put the small amount of money we'd saved for our honeymoon toward traveling to Croatia to knock on the doors of women's organizations. We had not been able to find an American organization that was willing to get involved. We were determined to help, so, three years after my arrival in the United States, Women for Women International was founded.

By 1995, Women for Women International was receiving help from hundreds of women all over the world. We called it a "sister to sister" way of helping. Every month, women survivors of war received thirty dollars and a letter from their sponsor; everything went directly to the women who needed help. That same year, I was honored for my humanitarian work by President Bill Clinton at a ceremony at the White House. Our work began to be featured in major media outlets, including on *The Oprah Winfrey Show* several times. Over the next eighteen years, Women for Women International became one of the largest women's organizations in America, raising and distributing more than 100 million dollars to almost half a million women survivors of wars internationally, including Nabintu, whose story, once I shared it, did indeed grip the hearts of many people who wanted to help.

I was proud of my work and happy to be helping in such a meaningful way, but life could still be very challenging. During the first decade of my humanitarian work, my mother fell ill. I helped her to secure the necessary documents to bring her to the United States for treatment, and we quickly learned that she had ALS, an incurable degenerative disease. The truth was stark: she was dying, and she would never return to Iraq except to be buried. It was then that she began telling me our story, hers and mine. I started to understand why she had rushed me to America: she hadn't liked the way Saddam had been eyeing me and commenting on me. Knowing what he had done to women—how many, many women he had raped—she did whatever it took to get her only daughter out, even when it risked our relationship. She knew Saddam would extend no favors to our family.

Perhaps the best gift my mother gave me was the truth. I had felt so angry and betrayed by her—the woman I loved the most. Why had she insisted that I marry and leave Iraq? Why had she left me all alone in the United States as a young woman to be abused by a stranger? Now we were taking steps toward healing. Now I understood that she had done everything she could to protect me. As life was slowly fading from her, she wrote out more details to fill in the gaps in our lives and to break the years of silence between us. Finally, I saw that the very act I thought of as my mother's betrayal was instead a clear sign of her courage, love, and determination to save me. She also helped me realize that people don't resist dictatorship and oppression only in big, heroic actions; they also resist in small, day-to-day actions. In this way, patiently and diligently, bit by bit, they protect their families and keep their children alive and safe. That's what my mother and father had done for me.

In death, my mother also gave me the chance to reunite with the rest of my family. When I took her body back to Iraq, I saw my father and youngest brother for the first time in almost a decade. I did not recognize them. My father had aged and taken up prayer beads. He was different from the secular man I grew up with. Now, he turned to God for relief from the terrible conditions he'd been living in through so many wars and so much destruction. My youngest brother, who had been a nine-year-old when I'd left, was a fully grown man now. It took time to create a new relationship, this time as adults.

I did not recognize the country either. It was 1999, and Iraqis were exhausted from lack of food and basic services like sanitation and medicines—the effect of years of sanctions. A million people had died since the first Gulf War had ended in 1991. By the time of my mother's funeral, everyone thought the worst was over. No one expected another war and unimaginable further destruction.

With a heavy heart, I returned to Iraq again in December 2002, on the eve of the second Gulf War. My youngest brother was now in danger of being drafted, and I needed to get him out. I also convinced my father to let me take the most valuable things from our family home. I'd learned from my work with victims of war what was most precious to survivors: birth, death, and education certificates, legal documents showing land ownership, and family photos. We had no idea what this second Gulf War would bring to Iraq, but if the country fell, the likelihood that our home would be pillaged was high. My father agreed.

The country did fall, and our house was pillaged. In fact, during the wars and the years of fighting that followed, my childhood home become many things that were beyond my imagination. Insurgent militias occupied our house for two years, first as an execution center and then, to disguise their activities from the Iraqi army, as a brothel. Neighbors tell us that trucks came regularly to collect all the bodies that militias were throwing into our garden—the same garden my father had so lovingly tended when I was a child. When the Iraqi army finally beat them out, the army itself made the house into a military base for yet another year.

Over this time, everything was ransacked. The waves of occupants took not only our furniture and china but even the electric wires from the walls. All that was left of the garden was one dry persimmon tree, its branches stripped of leaves. The land around it was completely barren. No one could have guessed that it had once been a lush green oasis, full of laughter, music, and dancing.

Almost a decade after the second Gulf War, the army returned the house to my family, and my father sold it to people we did not know. It was as if, after all that trauma, another house stood in its place, a ghost house. The history of my childhood, my parents' marriage, my mother's collections of art and fancy furniture, and my father's beautiful flowers and fruit trees had been desecrated, exterminated. It was clear that we could never live there again.

Still, I wanted to see the ruins of our family home for myself. On a trip to Baghdad in 2011, I drove to the Al Mansour neighborhood and knocked at the door. I needed to know if any part of the history of my life was still standing. A hesitant woman answered. I asked if I could see the room I grew up in. After a nervous pause, she invited me in. To my surprise, in my old room, I found a much younger girl also named Zainab. It is a common name in Iraq, but the symbolism was unmistakable. She was nine years old and wore her hair covered.

Two Zainabs, I thought to myself, *and two Iraqs*. When I was her age, I'd worn my hair loose and full of colorful hair clips. The household I'd grown up in had been secular and festive—it had a built-in bar and was known throughout our neighborhood for its parties. Anniversaries and birthdays were fully celebrated at our house. My window had looked out on the eucalyptus trees surrounding the cul-de-sac in front of our home.

This young Zainab was growing up in a house with religious flags hanging from the roof. She wore a hijab, a head scarf. Instead of eucalyptus trees outside, there were concrete walls, put up for protection shortly after the end of the war as security collapsed in the country. Across the cul-de-sac, the library where I used to do my homework had become a mosque. The Iraq of this young Zainab was all about sectorial and religious identity, about which tribe you belong to. The Iraq of my childhood had no room for what is Sunni and what is Shia, what is Muslim and what is Christian.

Now, when I saw the house, I saw a shell of what it used to be. I left thanking God that my mother did not have to see all these levels of destruction, of our home, our neighborhood, our country. If there was any part of me that, like her, enjoyed acquiring material things, this scene of my destroyed childhood home cured me of it. It was like a tattoo on my heart. Everything—all the beauty, all the prized possessions—had ended up as nothing, not even dust. All that was left were our stories.

✴

It is not easy to tell our stories. They carry our secrets, and I had buried mine deep in my consciousness. It was hard enough to admit that I'd been in an arranged marriage, and it was even harder to say that my first husband had raped me. But I had no idea that the hardest thing of all would be to expose the story I'd been trained never to tell—that of my family in Iraq.

Some stories may indeed be more extreme than others. Some women have been gang-raped, like Nabintu and her daughters, or sold into the sex trade or forced to live without basic rights and education. That doesn't mean that other women should not break their own silence and share their own stories. Just because you work in London or Silicon Valley does not mean that you should play down the abuses you endure. Some people may have been molested by a relative, and some have been verbally abused by a boss or a romantic partner. Some silence themselves to please those in power, even a relative or a colleague. Some allow themselves to be treated as sexual objects, thinking it will bring them a sense of acceptance, worth, and safety. The extremity of the stories might be more intense for a woman in Afghanistan than for a woman in Mississippi, but the essence—the abuse of power, the manipulation by fear, the stripping away of human dignity—is the same in both places. It is just cloaked by a different robe, dressed up in a different cut of cloth.

When we hide our stories, we isolate ourselves from the collective story. If we label the stories of "these poor people over *there*" as the only ones worth hearing, then we are assuming that we are totally free, without a shadow of our own, with nothing to expose or reconcile. We assign ourselves as the "saviors" and them as the "victims."

Each spirit struggles to be free, so each person's story has its own potency, and each situation extracts its own price. We show true respect for each other when we show up in the fullness of our own stories. Each story—no matter its severity or our privilege—has the full weight of emotion behind it. Our stories may be different, but their impact is undeniable, and we need to own them if we want to be free.

When my memoir was published in 2006, it got attention not just in America but in Iraq as well. I was worried that telling my truth would endanger my family, even though Saddam had been imprisoned and was in the midst of a trial that would eventually lead to his execution. What surprised me was the response the book got. It's true that my book put my father in a tough position—he was reinvestigated exhaustively by some militias and their leaders in Iraq until his innocence was once again proven. That process wasn't easy. At the same time, Iraqi men were calling him to express their gratitude: "Your daughter not only told her story, she told all of our stories. We are thankful to her." Young Iraqi women and men would stop me in the streets of London and New York to say, "Thank you for telling the world what happened to us Iraqis."

In America, I had feared that if people knew my connection to Saddam Hussein, they would stop seeing me and would see only him. He would steal my life again and erase my voice, my values, and all my humanitarian commitment. Instead, Americans were calling to say that they wished the book had been out before the United States had entered the Gulf Wars.

The more I shared my story, the more women from all walks of life started coming up to me in cafés, streets, and airports to tell me their own stories. At first I didn't know what to do when complete strangers would whisper intimate stories of molestation and abuse in my ears. Over time, I came to realize that Nabintu was right: when one person breaks her silence, she paves the path for others to break their own silence as well. We become witnesses of one another's stories, and in the process we give courage to one another.

If we all speak our truth, no matter how heavy or how trivial our stories seem, then together we can light the way toward a new future and a new story, one that is no longer based on silence and shame. I had locked my past into my heart for so many years that it had turned into a black stone, weighing heavily in the center of my chest. It suffocated me and sapped me of energy. But when I unlocked my secrets, that dark stone turned into a crystal: clear, transparent, and beautiful. In my utter vulnerability lay my protection and my power. No secrets, no hiding, no shame. When I took control of my story and willingly shared it with all, I felt that no one could hurt me anymore.

Now, whenever I hear a person speak their truth, even if it sheds light on the worst aspects of who they are, it always resonates with me and brings tears to my eyes. When told simply and honestly, the most terrible information carries courage, grace, and love. Whenever we tell our truth and break our silence, we become like candles that light the way for others out of their darkness until they find the courage to speak up themselves.

Only when we tell the truth can there be healing.

2

Living in Truth

Living our truth is not always easy,
but it is always worth it.

I t is hard to tell our truths to those we love. Yet the only way to understand what it takes to live and tell the truth is to experience it in the most intimate aspect of our lives. When we tell it to those closest to us—our parents, our siblings, our best friends, our spouses—we know the fears that come up, the courage we need to muster, and the risk required to create real change. We walk that journey and understand that it means being more compassionate than judgmental, more patient than frustrated.

When we're not ready to live our full truths, we are often attracted to people who can carry them for us. That goes on until we can embody those truths in ourselves. Have you ever wondered how a beautiful person could be with a plain-looking person, a chaotic person with someone calm and balanced, or why a generous person can be with someone stingy? This is true whether these people are husbands, wives, friends, siblings, neighbors, lovers, or colleagues. We are attracted to those who can carry a story that we cannot carry for ourselves, a characteristic, a strength, or a preference that we have not yet developed or allowed ourselves to admit or to express.

Amjad, my second husband, carried a story of kindness, safety, and love for me when I couldn't carry it in myself. When I first met him, I was a very vulnerable twenty-two-year-old, recently moved to Washington, DC. I had just escaped a brief and horrible first marriage to a man who'd turned abusive almost from the moment the ink dried on the marriage license. When I met Amjad, I was still very new to the United States, with no family or friends. I had moved into a new job, a new apartment, and a new life and vowed never to let any man touch me again. I didn't trust men at all. It took a couple of years, but Amjad's steady kindness allowed me to relax and feel safe again. Little by little, my fear and defensiveness melted away.

We call in the people we need. Maybe you yourself have looked back at a friendship or relationship with deep gratitude and awe or wondered how you ever loved a particular person or gotten so entangled in their world. They were carrying some story for you—and you for them.

Until I understood this, I could not understand how my friend Anna could have someone like Steve as her mentor and friend for such a long time. Anna was a successful CEO who led corporate teams and was highly sought after as a philanthropist. She had a strong humanitarian drive, and with it she inspired thousands of people to work toward ending injustices all over the world. In charge of so many people and such big visions, Anna had to project an image of confidence at all times. That meant she also needed help navigating her doubts and fears, as we all do.

Steve, her executive coach, was the one who listened to her small stories and carried their weight for her. He helped her process any vulnerability or discomfort she felt and to think through any tough decisions. With his charming French accent, he projected an air of cultured intelligence. No matter what he was saying, even when it was harsh, it seemed that it must be correct and sophisticated.

Anna needed Steve, yet they were polar opposites. If Anna was kind, warm, and forgiving, Steve was mean, controlling, and judgmental. If Anna was generous and inviting, Steve was miserly and cold. Where she made people feel at home and at ease, Steve would single people out in the most abrasive way and put them on the spot. He was not only blunt, he was also chauvinistic and competitive. He never let anyone forget that he was Anna's right-hand man.

For a decade, Steve accompanied Anna on her travels, helped her to run meetings, and over time started to co-run events with her. At first, protected by the sphere of Anna's love and generosity, Steve mistreated people behind Anna's back. Then, cautiously, he would do it in her presence. Over time, he felt completely comfortable mistreating people right in front of her.

If Anna noticed, she didn't say a thing. Hardly anyone dared to raise the issue with Anna. Instead, they tiptoed around Steve, concealing their dislike and distrust of him. Others stepped away quietly.

After working closely with Steve for so long, things began to shift. Anna began checking in with her closest friends about his behavior, opening the door for them to tell her what was really going on. Finally, at a breakfast meeting, Anna woke up.

As usual, Steve was very rude to someone at the meeting. "You are being very manipulative and abrasive," he said coldly to a female attendee. "You are lucky I'm not telling everyone what you told me an hour ago."

Anna encouraged the woman to stand up for herself: "Would you like to respond to Steve?"

"He is not worthy of my response," the woman replied. "I don't trust Steve. No one does." Another woman agreed, and another nodded her head. The minute the meeting ended, all the women started whispering, and the men started speaking up. There was nothing hidden now: Anna could not help but notice how deeply uncomfortable everyone was about Steve.

Later, in private, Anna invited Steve to explain himself. It was a turning point, not just in her relationship with her coach, but also in herself. The truth was, until then, she had struggled to say no to anyone. She could not bear to tell anyone to stop doing things she didn't agree with. It had always been easier for her to lead with kindness. So for years, she had made Steve create the boundaries, even in his abrasive way. He was always able to turn people down or hold them at bay when she couldn't do it for herself. He had no problem creating limits. He embodied her strength and courage until she could do it herself.

It took Anna ten years to be able to stop hiding behind Steve and letting him do her boundary-setting work for her. It took her all those years to find her true voice and be comfortable with it. When she found her strength and courage to set limits, she was still polite; she never adopted Steve's cruel manner. For his part, Steve did exactly the same with her. He hid behind her power and the love and respect others had for her. He borrowed her legitimacy until he could develop his own sense of importance separately from her and the business opportunities that being associated with her had provided.

After all those years of love and trust, Steve rejected Anna's claim that he was not appropriate at the meeting. He avoided any further encounters with her. That conversation was the last they ever had. Anna didn't have the chance to discuss anything more with him or formally say good-bye. He simply disappeared.

That shift from being attracted to certain qualities in others to becoming able to embody those qualities in ourselves is not an easy one. It entails moving from dependence to independence; from hiding aspects of ourselves to showing up in all aspects of ourselves; from denying our shadows to seeing them, accepting them, and integrating them. That process can bring on soul searching, a sorting through of what is our own truth and what is someone else's. It can be full of strong emotions and tough questions. When we haven't done it before, it can feel very surprising, like we're peeling away a layer in ourselves that we didn't know was there.

We all have a choice in how we want to live, but we don't always ask ourselves this question directly. How *do* we want to live? We can live a life of fear, our hearts going numb and some part of us dying. Or we can live a life of truth and love, which involves another kind of risk—the risk of making ourselves vulnerable and uncomfortable, and maybe being judged, or even hurting others or losing relationships. It is worth it, though, because when we are brave, what we are risking is being true to ourselves and becoming free.

I also had to face this choice. It took time and many mistakes to realize that choosing to live in truth was worth it. What I realized was that the taste of freedom was so delicious, it made the hard journey of walking in truth worth every moment. It was worth risking the life I had once cherished in order to discover the life that was waiting for me.

*

For years, it was normal for me to experience waves of tears or spasms of anxiety, to not be able to breathe fully, to suffer moments of anger and pain, or to become obsessed with work, pouring all my energy into it. That's where I hid, in all these extremes. The truth was that shame was eating me from within. I was ashamed to tell the story of my past, ashamed to reveal that I was not as strong as the image I projected, and over time, I became ashamed of feeling estranged from the man I had loved deeply and with whom I had once had a most beautiful relationship—my own husband.

In my mind, Amjad and I were the perfect couple. He was what I wanted in a man: patient, loving, and intelligent. We loved each other and supported each other to realize our dreams in the world. He introduced me to life in America and to parts of American culture that I had no idea about, such as science fiction and *Star Trek*. He was always interested in my work and helped me launch Women for Women International.

Amjad was also a full partner at home. If I cooked, he washed up. If I did the laundry, he did the ironing. If I got upset with him, he responded with calmness. He walked the walk of partnership without me ever having to ask him to step up. He was always generous and giving, too: whenever he had a little extra money, he'd spend it on something nice for me, like a dress or a book. Hand in hand, we survived the challenges of young married life: the financial hardships of being students, the pressure of working and studying at the same time, the distress of illness in our families, and the pressures of our early careers. We were always each other's loves. I would kiss him with eyes open and know I was kissing the love of my life.

After nine years, we thought that our marriage was strong enough for us to take time and space to pursue our individual interests separately for a year. I wanted to get my master's degree in developmental studies at the London School of Economics, and Amjad wanted to join a Palestinian-Israeli peace negotiation in the Middle East. We would come back to the United States after that one year and take our marriage to a new phase, building a home and maybe having a child.

Before that, Amjad and I were one of these couples that did everything together. We were inseparable, like two peas in a pod. Since I knew no one in America, Amjad and his family and friends took me in. I felt protected by them as well as included and loved by them. So Amjad and I had the same friends and hobbies. We cooked together, worked out together, went to bed at the same time. We often laughed that we did everything as a "we," never as "me" and "you."

When I started my course in London and he moved to Palestine, it was the first time in very a long time that each of us was exploring the "I" in "me." After nine years of marriage, I had forgotten what it meant to explore new things in life or politics without sharing it with my husband. I hadn't gone shopping alone, or developed new friendships separate from him, or gone out without him by my side since we got married.

Amjad was doing the same thing, too. Also, he had never lived outside America, let alone in a war zone. He was learning what it was like to work for peace in a very politicized environment. He had to worry about water shortages and curfews and Israeli checkpoints, and to live without relief from the constant threat of violence.

At first, we were very excited about all of our new findings. We would call every day and share everything with each other. But over time, he got busy at work, and I got busy with school, and both of us got busy with our new social lives. The year passed well. But when it was time for us to return to the United States and resume our family life as we had planned, Amjad made a request: he wanted to stay in his job for one more year. That would mean another year of living separately.

When you love a person, truly, you get joy from seeing him thrive in whatever he does. Amjad was thriving and was happy. Out of complete love for him, I wanted him to continue. I said, "Of course."

I returned alone to the United States and resumed my humanitarian work at Women for Women International. Our second year living apart was not nearly as easy as the first. Our individual explorations continued, but we were no longer as excited to share them. When we visited every few months, either me going to Palestine or him coming back to Washington, each of us felt like strangers to the other's experience. I had lived and worked in war zones almost my entire life. I knew about the hardships people suffered, so I was no longer patient with Amjad when he shared his experiences with me. Amjad, for his part, couldn't connect with my new friends or my new interest in dressing up and going out dancing, things we had not done as a "we" before.

Irritated by our different interests, we bickered more. Or, rather, I picked at things, and he said nothing. We also stuck to the familiar parts of our lives in an effort to stabilize ourselves: we went to bed together, woke up together, shared breakfast, and chitchatted about the day's news. But our conversations became about logistical things—did you pay that bill or send that gift and so on. In the evenings, when he was home visiting from Palestine, rather than being alone together again, we'd meet other people for dinner. We had a lot of close friends to catch up with, but we were also avoiding facing this development in our relationship.

It was a confusing time. Silence started to sneak into a space between us where there had never been any silence before. I knew I loved my husband. I also knew that my heart was getting colder and that I was becoming sad. As I explored more in my life without Amjad, I felt my love starting to slip away, yet I did not know how to articulate my feelings. I started gaining weight as an expression of my unhappiness, just a few pounds, but enough to make my clothes uncomfortable, like an expression of stress that swelled up from within. Words can lie but not the body.

More alarming was that once Amjad had gone back to his work in Palestine, I also started noticing my attraction to other men. When I am in love, I don't see anyone else. But that was changing. When I realized what was happening, I knew I had to pay attention to the state of my marriage. I couldn't wait any longer for Amjad to finish his second year in the West Bank. I needed to be with my husband again as soon as possible.

"I am hanging on by the tips of my fingers," I said. "If you want to save our marriage, you need to come back soon."

Amjad moved back to the United States a month or two later. I knew he was making a big sacrifice for us, but when he walked through the door of the new apartment that I had rented, he also seemed like a stranger. I was so familiar with the way he looked, the way he walked, his mannerisms, his scent, but I had no idea who *this* man was. He seemed to feel the same way about me, but he also seemed less troubled by the new distance.

Determined to stay together, we tried to rewind to the time when our hearts had been talking to each other effortlessly. Both of us remembered how that felt, how we had acted, what the other had liked, what had made us laugh. We did all those things again, hoping to trigger the feelings we had had. Amjad, for example, bought me the same flavor of yogurt that I had loved when we first got married. Back then, this gesture had always made me happy. Eleven years later, I no longer liked blueberry yogurt. Yet, no matter how many times I told him, he always bought it when he went to the store. As he emptied the grocery bag, I would be both touched and frustrated. He was trying to do what he knew how to do, but he was not able to hear that I no longer wanted it.

We were like two actors trying to repeat an old play of true love hoping that if we acted it well enough, it would become as real as it had once been. We filled our time working and seeing family and friends, but our lives were moving separately. I was going to more self-development retreats, reflecting on who I was, what I wanted, and what my strengths and weaknesses were. I had new friends and new interests. I begged Amjad to come camping with me or to join me on a spiritual retreat. I wanted to dig deep into myself, and I wanted him to be a part of it or at least to witness the experience with me as a way of creating a common bond that we could grow within. I thought he would find it interesting, too. For his part, he became more and more consumed with his peace-negotiating work and involved with his new friends in politics and in the diplomatic world. They say anyone who works on the Palestine-Israel problem becomes obsessed with it, and that was certainly happening in our household.

Together but separate was our new rhythm—except that he still saw the together part while I was seeing the separate part. When I started using "I," he would correct me: "It's 'we,' Zainab."

But more and more I felt that there was no "we."

Amjad and I loved each other, but the relationship wasn't the same. It was like living on top of a reservoir without understanding how to get access to the water. After a decade of loving marriage, I was now standing much more on my own two feet. I wasn't a vulnerable girl anymore; I had different needs and desires now. The truth is we change. As we change, the dynamic in our relationship changes—it has to accommodate this person we are becoming, for better or for worse. When we are true to ourselves, we grapple with these changes. When we are afraid, we hide from them and sometimes also hide from the very people we love. This makes us live in half-truths. When we can't stand even to live in the half-truths, we act out.

✳

Ours was not the only way of struggling. In fact, there is no perfect formula for finding or living in truth in friendships or relationships. There are those who explore the difficulties and changes together, no matter what comes. There are also those who deny the truth for as long as they can and even then squeeze their eyes shut when it's all but impossible to ignore.

It's about wrangling with truth. It's about how familiar we are with our own truth, how comfortable we are expressing it, and how much we are already living it. Some people fill that space of struggle with loud and anguished screams or with silent screams that go inward, unheard. Some wrestle with their truth by doing therapy, reading books, or watching movies. Others search for it outside their relationship, by having affairs, going to prostitutes, hoarding secrets, or looking to stimulants, intrigue, or danger to fill that space. Some wait until a disaster pushes them into clarity, and others, until the brink of death. Still others never get there.

The journey from the awareness of what's true for us *now* to the telling of that truth can be a messy one. It can feel lonely or confusing to wonder how in the world we arrived at this point. How could things have changed so much? What part of us still loves our old life? What part of us does not? What part of us is angry? Afraid? Insecure? Can our identity and our sense of purpose—and our relationship—survive this?

Laurie and Michael were both attractive, breezy artists who lived and worked in Arizona, traveled all over the world making films, and followed a healthy lifestyle. They'd fallen in love in their twenties, married, and had kids. One day, a couple of decades into their marriage, Laurie was picking up a visiting artist from the local airport and, to her surprise, sparks started flying. With his long hair and sandals, his tattoos and woven bracelets, he reminded her of Michael when they'd first met.

Laurie stayed in touch with the younger artist. She was flirting with him, and he was flirting back. It's natural to feel attracted to others over the course of a marriage, but when there's a strong urge to act on that attraction, it's time to pay attention. Laurie caught herself. She knew it wasn't about him. It was about what was—or was no longer—happening in her marriage.

"We need to wake up," Laurie told Michael. "If we stay like this our marriage will end. But if there is still love between us, then we have a chance."

At first, they explored separately. *Do I go? Do I stay? Do I love him? Do I leave her? What am I doing? What do I want?* After going to therapy and seeking out spiritual masters individually for some time, they were strong enough to explore these questions together. As they explored why and how they'd drifted apart, buried issues from Michael's childhood started to surface, and then Laurie's own deeper stories also came up. She saw him crying; he saw her in pain. It was not easy. At times, their needs and truths seemed too different to be compatible anymore and pushed them right up to the edge of a more permanent separation. Their saving grace was that no matter how painful things were, they continued to talk and hold each other's hands through the entire bumpy journey.

After a few years of this struggle, they hardly expected to make it as a couple. They had tried separating, they had weathered a family crisis, they had done lots of self-work both individually and together. They were amazed to realize that their love was still intact after all of these ups and downs. They came out the other side of their turmoil with a renewed, more mature love and a relationship that was just as passionate as the one from decades ago. Now it also bore witness to them as fully complex humans, each with a history. It allowed for pain and struggle, for ambivalence and confusion, and for tears and laughter. It became much more accepting.

Laurie and Michael walked through their fire together. Not everyone does. There are also those people who hide their struggle in the status quo, like my friend Annabelle did. Annabelle was a joyful, larger-than-life women's rights activist from San Francisco. She had a huge laugh and constantly filled her home with people and events—fundraisers, lectures, and all kinds of gatherings. She loved to entertain.

Annabelle had married a successful businessman twenty years before I met her and had dedicated herself to helping others. No one around her seemed to know much about her reclusive husband, a tall, sturdily built man who hardly said a word. We knew that where Annabelle was buoyant and energetic, he often seemed depressed and disengaged, but she never made a big deal of their differences and only complained in passing about their marital problems. He'd float through the events at their house, drink in hand, like a ghost. She'd mention his drinking but quickly brush it away with a smile and then change the subject.

"I have so much gratitude for everything else around me," she would say.

Then, one day, while Annabelle was traveling around the world in support of one of her nonprofit organizations, her husband threw out her treasured collection of inspirational writings. Annabelle was an enthusiast about keeping all things she liked since she was a child. She'd keep a candy wrapper if it had a quote she liked. Her box contained snippets of poems and sayings that she loved, photographs from parties she'd thrown, journals, and all kinds of happy keepsakes. She liked to pull the box out now and then to browse, read, savor, and reflect. When she discovered that the beloved box was missing, she was devastated.

"It was all junk," her husband said when she confronted him. "I just threw out the junk." Yet he knew what the collection meant to her.

More than his years of drinking, more than his silence toward her or the depression he'd withdrawn into, it was this simple yet cruel act that woke Annabelle up. She had tolerated his slide downward, his retreating away from her. She had overlooked it, as we all overlook things in long relationships. This time, however, she was hurt, really hurt. She had reached her limit. She realized how deeply disappointed she was in him and in their marriage. His cruel act was like a mirror in which she could not help but see her reflection.

"Do I leave, or do I stay?" Annabelle asked her close friends.

Annabelle knew that leaving him would mean making a radical change in her life and her lifestyle. It would have its own costs, some of them big. So when her best friend told her not to worry about it, just stay together and things would work out, she was ready to be persuaded.

"As long as he supports you and leaves you alone to do whatever you want," said her friend, "who cares what he does?! Stay in the marriage and ignore him."

Annabelle took that advice. She made a practical decision: she would coexist with her husband in exchange for the nice life he provided—the beautiful home, the luxury travel, and the life of a wealthy socialite that she put to good use. She put on a façade of "everything is okay," just like she'd put on her bright red lipstick before one of her fabulous events.

I never heard her speak of the marriage or her husband again. Her husband went back to his drinking, and she went back to all her social activities. It was as if somewhere inside she had left him mentally and emotionally, while physically she stayed married. She became even more active in supporting campaigns for women's rights around the world. It was easier for her to talk passionately about the struggles of women in Africa or the Middle East than to face her own struggle to live in her own truth every day.

Then came the twist of fate. A few years later, she was diagnosed with cancer and given a few months to live. When life became a matter of months, not years, she got very clear about what she would no longer accept. She asked her husband to leave. She wanted to spend the last moments of her life in her truth, surrounded only by the people she loved the most. He respected her wishes and stepped away. Three months later, she died.

Annabelle had waited until nearly the very last breath of her life to stop tolerating the lie that she was living. The question is: how long do we want to wait to declare what we know, to stand by it, live it, and be free in it?

Amjad and I neither explored the challenges in our relationship together, like Laurie and Michael did, nor did we surrender to the silence that was creeping into our hearts, as Annabelle had.

"Before you make any final decision," a friend advised me, "you must try to save your marriage by every means possible. You don't want to have any regrets if you end up leaving."

I heard his wisdom. Amjad and I had such a strong, loving history that I couldn't just give up. I felt I owed Amjad a debt for all the happy years he had given me. He'd saved me when I was vulnerable. When I feared men, he melted my heart with kindness. With him, I had learned to trust. Above all, I did not want to hurt him.

So I committed to trying anything and everything. I repeated, "I love him, I love him, I love him" in my heart, trying with my will alone to reignite my love and passion. I organized a second honeymoon to a romantic place. I redecorated our bedroom. I asked Amjad to join me on my adventures in nature, and I found a marriage counselor for us. At times, Amjad saw all these new explorations as the things that were taking me away from him. At other times, he was just too busy with work to join me. He also thought that the old, familiar routine of our lives worked fine. He ultimately thought that we'd come through this rough patch okay.

Maybe, I thought, we should follow through on our plan to have a child. Maybe the energy of a new life would bring us closer. Back home in Iraq, women would often say, "Have a baby and save the marriage." What they meant, I came to realize, was not "save" the marriage but "lock in" the marriage, locking a husband and wife into a mutual obligation toward their child. I didn't want to lock Amjad or myself into anything; I wanted us to live authentically together. In truth, I had never wanted a child. My condition of marrying Amjad was that we would not have kids—a deal he agreed to even though he wanted them. I realized I was acting in crazed desperation: bringing children into an unhappy relationship would be a disaster.

What I didn't know was that when we don't tell the truth—the simple, honest, unfiltered truth—about what we feel inside our hearts, the feelings we are trying to hide get even more potent. The pain becomes more painful, the loneliness becomes lonelier, the sadness becomes much sadder. My unhappiness grew because I was afraid to say the simple truth: I was staying in the marriage out of loyalty to a very good man, but my heart was not happy anymore.

In my unhappiness, frustration, and confusion, I eventually became cruel toward Amjad. I would speak with friends in my native Arabic, knowing he would not understand the nuances of the conversations or the jokes or the music. In this way, I subtly isolated him. I would make cruel remarks about things that only a wife could know would hurt her husband. I was impatient with him and was not attentive when he shared childhood traumas that were surfacing. When he asked for advice related to his work, I didn't respond. I was not interested. At the same time, I questioned his love for me and became suspicious of him if he showed kindness toward another woman. My cruelty became the norm. The more I indulged it, the colder and more reckless I became in taking his love for granted.

If love is about showing up, then I was no longer showing up, either for him or for myself. If love is about being present and seeing what the other person is going through and communicating through it, then I stopped being present. I didn't have the courage to tell him what was inside my heart, nor could I push myself to confront my own silence. Unable to acknowledge that I was unhappy, I acted out.

I became ugly. I was ugly in my behavior toward the man I loved.

When we avoid the truth to spare other people, our silence becomes a sharper knife that cuts deeper. Our silence hurts others. We cause harm even as we think we are avoiding it.

Before she'd died, Annabelle had invited a group of close friends to visit her in San Francisco. We were bunch of girlfriends hanging out, laughing, ordering in Italian food. Annabelle gave us each a private session with a Tarot card reader. In the Qur'an there is a line that says, "Fortune-tellers lie even when they are telling the truth." I believe this, too, because no matter how psychic people are, no one can know the ultimate truth. Even though I was doubtful about this way of gaining insight, I still couldn't resist exploring the mysterious unknown. I made an appointment.

The Tarot card reader started by shuffling the cards. She asked me to pull a number of them and spread them out on the table between us. When she turned them over and took a look, she said, "Oh, you are single."

"No, I am married," I corrected her.

She apologized, shuffled again, and again asked me to pull several cards. She looked again: "It says you are alone and not in a relationship."

"No, no, I am a married woman," I corrected her again.

We went through the process one more time, and yet again, the cards said the same thing. I started crying. This time I understood: "I am married, yes, but I am indeed alone." It was the first time I could admit this truth.

The day we utter the truth out loud is the day we are confronted with choices. Everything shifts. We must decide which actions to take and which not to take; if we are going to face this truth and do something about it or if we are going to deny it, turn away, and begin to die a little bit from within.

When I came home after my visit with Annabelle, I sat on my sofa and cried. I had finally acknowledged my truth about me and Amjad, but I did not know what to do about it yet. I knew from writing my memoir that although the journey of truth is a hard one, it is worth walking. Only when I told the truth in my life could I put down the heavy burden I was carrying and stop hiding from myself and from life.

I was still crying on the couch when Amjad came home. When he saw my tears, he knew. "You want to leave me, don't you?"

I held my head in my hands and nodded. *Yes.*

It was Amjad's courage, not mine, that allowed me to articulate what was true, as painful as that was. When truth is out in the open, it creates a bridge we can walk across to each other despite our walls and defenses. For the first time in a very long while, we sat down together. That day in our living room, with our favorite music playing in the background, we meditated together. Then, gently, slowly, we started talking. We could finally talk authentically about our lives, our marriage, and each other. We did it without blame. We owned our words, actions, and inactions. I knew that in acting out rather than simply telling him the truth of my feelings, I had risked losing Amjad's love and respect. I was lucky;

Amjad was (and still is) very kind to me. He knew my soul was longing for new explorations in my life, a deeper understanding of myself and the freedom that I had tasted by writing out the truth about my past.

A few days later, after we had talked openly and honestly with each other, Amjad packed and left. The depth of our respect and love for each other was never in question; we knew we would always be friends. We also knew that was the end of what had been for the longest time a very loving relationship.

After he left, I found myself spending more time at the house, in the garden and the kitchen, planting flowers and trying out new recipes. The last few years that we'd lived together, I'd filled my schedule with travel and meetings. I wasn't consciously avoiding Amjad; I'd thought my work required me to be that busy.

When Amjad came to visit a couple of months later, he found me cooking and gardening, happy and at peace.

"I can see that now you are happy," he said, noticing my newfound smile. "My biggest act of love for you, Zainab, is to let you go. That is how much I love you."

I was touched by his words and, as ever, by the generosity of his love—I could see that he was in a lot of pain.

The day we carry our own story for ourselves is the day we start to renegotiate our relationships with those who have been carrying it for us. In the case of Amjad and me, we didn't know how to evolve together inside our marriage. So we left the marriage and evolved our relationship into a close and mature friendship instead.

Less than a year later, Amjad and I went to divorce court. It would be a lie to say I had no sadness about the end of this relationship. Amjad had become my best teacher in unconditional love—before marriage, during marriage, and after marriage. It was bittersweet to let him go. When we met for dinner the night before our court date, I gave him a gift of an empty box made of black painted wood. We did not hug or cry but looked at each other with love and sadness. "May this new box be filled with our new friendship and continued respect, love, and admiration for each other," I said.

We had already divided our things, offering to each other whatever we wanted to take. There were no disputes. We both wanted to be generous and prioritize our love and respect for each other over all the other feelings that arose in the process. We navigated the inevitable moments of annoyance and irritation as sensitively as we could.

The next day, we entered the divorce court holding hands. The judge looked surprised: "Aren't you getting divorced?"

When I said yes, she directed us to stand opposite each other, in two separate aisles. "Are you sure?" she repeated. I nodded. Then, she proclaimed our divorce final.

✳

Living our truth is the way to freedom. That doesn't mean that everyone will like it. When we discover what is true for us and what is not true, people who've grown accustomed to knowing us in a certain way may not want to deal with who we are becoming. It might challenge their ideas too much, ideas about us and about themselves.

Facing my truth regarding my marriage was hard, very hard. Sharing the news of our separation and divorce with our friends and family presented its own set of challenges. These intimate conversations triggered different reactions. There were those who held our pain and our stories with love and respect, without judgment. Our families, who had loved us both very much, asked over and over again if we were sure about separating but ultimately supported us in our decision.

Others were not so supportive. Some were sad and disappointed, seeing the breakup of our marriage as the end of a relationship they had idealized, almost like the end of love itself. Some were critical, blaming me for daring to want something different than a wonderful man like Amjad. Some acquaintances tried to seduce him as soon as he moved out, and others did the same to me. Some people gossiped and tried to create friction between us.

Among those who were angry and destructive was my friend Margret. Over lunch, I shared with her what I'd gone through to arrive at my decision. She asked more and more questions, becoming like a prosecutor who had me on the stand. Finally, with a powerful mixture of anger and resentment, she said sarcastically, "Well, this is *very* courageous of you."

I couldn't understand her irritation. I was even more confused when she later called Amjad to gossip about me. He called me right after: "Zainab, there are people trying to divide us. I just want to let you know that I see through it. Our relationship is the most important thing to me." It wasn't long before my friendship with Margret dissolved completely.

It took me a while to understand that when one person dares to tell her own truth, it becomes like a mirror to others' lives, reflecting the degree of truth they are living in. What complex web of lies and deceptions—and self-deceptions—are woven into their lives?

Margret's anger was not really about my separation from Amjad. It was more a reflection of whatever challenges she was going through in her own marriage that she couldn't bear to look at. Her anger showed that I had touched her, irritated her, and unintentionally pointed out something uncomfortable about her own life.

Whether we live our life fully or fail to live it is our responsibility alone. It is our own life, our own breath, and our own joy that are at stake. It was my responsibility to be in truth to myself and to Amjad. Failing to do that was failing myself.

✱

After my truth was told and my divorce was final, it was time to be alone again. I had been with Amjad for most of my adult life outside of Iraq, and it was time to find out who I was now without him. I called a friend who had extended an open invitation to stay in her house in Mexico. "Stay there as long as you need," she said graciously. "Stay until you get your spirit back."

Two days later, I was there.

It was beautiful. The house had a pool and was surrounded by lush gardens. Most importantly, it was quiet, with no one around. For the first week, I did nothing but cry, eat, and sleep. As I began to emerge from my cocoon, easing myself back into existence, I read through her bookshelf of inspiring books about women, nature, activism, and change. I did yoga, meditated for hours at a time, walked on the empty beach, and indulged myself with as much sleep as I needed. Creativity started to bubble up inside me. I found some watercolors and started painting for the first time in my life. Words started pouring out in a torrent of poetic images. I felt more alive than I had in years.

One day, on one of my long walks on the empty white-sand beach, I felt like dancing. Alone on the sand, without anybody around, I whirled around and around in utter joy. I felt so happy! That is when I realized, it is me—*I am the cake of my own happiness.* No one could take this happiness away from me, nor could anyone give it to me. Whoever came into my life would be the icing on this cake, but I would always be the cake itself.

After only a few weeks of living so quietly and allowing myself to rest, explore, and create, I felt grounded in my own truth, freedom, and joy, things that I had been searching for outside of myself for years. It had been so easy to busy myself with work rather than address the needs and impulses that had been bubbling up inside me. As I packed my bags to go home, I knew I would have to make some changes in my work life, although I didn't know exactly what those would be. I just knew that I wanted to stay more in that sense of joy that had grown so effortlessly when I'd gotten quiet.

When I returned from Mexico, my breath was fuller and deeper. I was able to *be* without the burden of living in a lie anymore. It made everything more peaceful. But this wasn't the end of my journey. In fact, it was the beginning. Once I had more ground under my feet, knew more about who I was and what made me happy, a more startling awareness started to rise up within me. This awareness showed me I had more work to do if I truly wanted to live in truth in every part of my life.

It was a Sunday night, and I was at home alone. I was feeling restless, unable to settle down and get quiet. To distract myself, I tried to tidy up. That didn't work. So I busied myself with reading. That also didn't work. I was uncomfortable in my own skin. It was like I had an itch I couldn't scratch.

Suddenly, it occurred to me: If Amjad had been with me, I would have picked on something he'd said or done to irritate me, and I would have blamed him. I would have caused a fight. But he was not around: the house was empty, my room was empty, and the bed I was lying on held only me.

That's when it happened. I saw my own finger—the one that used to point at Amjad—pointing back at me, accusing me.

Oh no, I thought. *It is me!*

For the first time in my life, I realized that instead of facing myself, my habit was to point my finger at the person right in front of me and blame him for my restlessness and dissatisfaction. He wasn't paying enough attention, he wasn't hearing me, he didn't care, he was doing things wrong, et cetera, et cetera.

My mind began to fill with whispers of the pain and frustration I had projected not only onto Amjad but also onto family, friends, and colleagues, making them all the source of my discontent. I realized that if I wanted to keep tasting the delicious truth, joy, and freedom in my life, I had to follow my own finger and look inward at what it was pointing at. A year after my divorce, I was confronted with what I had left before me: the mother of all journeys, the one that went deeply inward, the journey into myself.

3

Owning Our Success

Our dreams do not
require us to self-sacrifice.

hen we get quiet and allow ourselves to just *be*, our urgent questions are often answered. That can be counterintuitive for people who are driven and analytical or who spend a lot of time in their heads. But the answers are there, deep within our beings, if we can just find the time and space to tune into them. When I was struggling with my role at work, I knew I needed to get quiet and listen for answers. At first, I just wasn't sure how to access that quiet or hear my deepest wisdom.

At that moment, I was receiving high-profile awards and press coverage for my humanitarian work. I was forty-one years old and had been building Women for Women International since I was twenty-three. In that time, Women for Women International had grown from a small operation with my then-husband, Amjad, and a handful of volunteers working out of my in-laws' basement into a major American humanitarian organization with seven hundred staff members and offices in ten countries. We were now helping hundreds of thousands of women survivors of wars and distributing millions of dollars in aid. My role had evolved from meeting one-on-one with women in conflict areas to driving the organization's fundraising efforts. Women for

Women International had done a *lot* of good in the world, but even with all of this achievement, inside I felt like a failure.

To me, whatever we were accomplishing did not feel good enough or big enough to have the kind of impact I envisioned. I wanted the world to *hear*, truly hear, the voices, thoughts, and views of women survivors of war and poverty, not just feel bad for them. These women might not be educated or articulate, but they had true wisdom to share. The world, though, seemed to prefer seeing their destitution, torn clothes, devastated faces, blood and dirt. Pity raised money, I found, but it did not get women's voices heard, dignity seen, or strength witnessed. I wanted people not just to give money once they'd seen the horrific images and heard the terrible stories but to listen more deeply and change their own stereotypes about these women. That was the answer to eradicating women's suffering globally, I was sure. The shift in attitudes was not happening fast enough.

My feelings of frustration and failure embarrassed me deeply. I did not want to admit them to anyone, not to my mentors, colleagues, or friends, not even to my therapist. I could articulate them only in the privacy of my own thoughts, but most of the time my mind was racing. I was restless and uncomfortable, without enough room to contemplate much. Perhaps to avoid a deeper encounter with my own heart, I overbooked myself with work and social activities.

Finally, even distracting myself became irritating. It was time to explore my feelings further. To do that, I needed the safety of silence. Not knowing anything about Zen meditation, I booked myself into a four-day retreat. I didn't know what I was getting myself into; I just knew that the center was reputable and that I would be observing my thoughts as I sat and walked in the meditation halls and in the woods with the other participants, whom I did not know. Anonymity, quiet, and the unfamiliar setting in a beautiful, stately house in the woods would provide a safe place for me to ruminate. It sounded perfect.

On the first day, I experienced a torrent of painful feelings, all of which I wanted to avoid. I had meditated at home before, following tips from friends or yoga classes or videos I had seen online, but just for ten minutes at a time. As I sat for hours on the small, round cushions on the floor that first day, every part of my body ached. My mind rebelled. I fixated on other participants' every movement to try to distract myself from going inward. When someone sighed or sneezed or shifted their body, I noticed. It was easier to pay attention to the details of the pattern in the carpet or the sound of the copper bell that marked the time than to ask myself the questions I came to ask.

Eventually, my body settled and relaxed, and the silence took over. I started to forget about all the little distracting habits of the people around me on their own cushions. I finally dared to hear my own thoughts and engage in an inner conversation. *Why are you so uncomfortable inside?* I asked myself. A flood of feelings washed over me: I was ashamed of articulating my feelings of failure so publicly.

Why shame? I asked, allowing for the most honest thought to answer back. It was the shame of missing my mark, of doing more talking than accomplishing; the shame of not being as successful as my successful friends; the worry that people might feel bad for me or look down on me or that I might have to give up on my big dreams and just be content with what I had accomplished so far. I was also afraid to live with this restless discontent for the rest of my life. I had so much more I wanted to do. What if I just couldn't do it? Was I working hard enough? Was I doing the best job I could? Was I pushing as hard as I could? Giving all I had?

By day two, I was checking into every corner of my mind. I wanted to see all the questions that were arising from different angles. I allowed myself to hear each thought and feel each feeling fully—the doubt, the shame, the sadness, the worry, the anxiety, the embarrassment, everything. Going through them all was like going through a storage room full of clutter. I checked inside thoughts and feelings like I would check inside an old box, taking the insight I needed and throwing out the rest. If worry came, I checked out why I was worried. What was the story behind the worry? Where did it come from? Was it real or not real? I stayed with the feeling until I had processed and digested it, and then I let it go.

When day three arrived, my mind was finally empty. I had explored everything until there were no more feelings and no more clutter, no more questions and no more answers. I had worked through my restlessness and my desire to accomplish more than I was currently able to do. Inside, I felt only silence. My inner landscape was like the beautiful snowy woods outside—quiet, except for occasional small sounds around me. I had no thoughts and no feelings. My mind was not talking anymore. I was released from my attachments about who I actually was or felt I was supposed to be. Nothing mattered in that silence.

Our attachments to whom we think we're supposed to be are like chains around our necks. Our identities get wrapped up in the external roles, titles, and accomplishments that we put value on, especially when it comes to our work. A wealthy businessman values how much he's worth financially. A research scientist values the cure she is working on. A writer values the books he writes and publishes. In my case, I valued how much social change I could create through my advocacy for women's rights and my humanitarian work.

At first, it might seem that one pursuit or identity *is* more valuable than another. Surely, the cure for a disease is more important than how many books an author sells. Surely, creating social change that improves thousands—if not millions—of lives is more important than increasing the wealth of one individual. At a fundamental level, though, no matter what our vocation is, our accomplishments are where we find our core self-value and feel affirmed.

Attachments are attachments, I realized, no matter who we are or what we identify with. When we value ourselves because of *what* we accomplish and *how much* we accomplish, our souls are forever held hostage to these attachments. No matter how much we do, how many dollars we accumulate, cures we discover, books we sell, or people we help, it is never going to be enough to permanently fulfill us.

The world may think I had made it, but if my measure of success had no end point, I would never reach the pinnacle of success in my own mind. This meant that no matter how much I was doing, how hard I was working, how many women I helped, or how much funding I secured, it was never going to be enough. I was completely identified with my work, and in my own mind, I could never be successful enough at it. That was a very big chain around my soul, a huge weight on my being. Realizing this was like cutting the umbilical cord to my shame.

On the fourth day of the retreat, my soul danced freely in a space without boundaries. I felt joy for no reason and for every reason. I did not care about who I was or what I had accomplished or not accomplished. My worries related to my work were no longer heavy. All I felt was a sense of limitlessness in myself, a pure lightness of being without any expectations. Everything felt possible.

When I got home from the retreat, out of the woods and back into the city, I was again plunged into the driving pressure to do, accomplish, succeed, compete, and work hard. One short silent retreat couldn't instantly change the shape of my life—or my mind. It had just given me a taste of what freedom from attachments could be like. It was like tasting chocolate for the first time: we can't describe how good it tastes until we've actually tasted it, and then we can't ever forget that taste. Now that I had seen the source of my pain and the route to my freedom, I had a clear path to follow.

My first step was to talk with friends about my feelings of shame and failure. In exposing our secrets, I was discovering, we release ourselves from their grip. These conversations brought up more questions: What does success really mean? Why do we talk so often about it as a worthwhile goal but avoid talking about the pain and challenges we encounter along the way? The world celebrates success. It also tends to glamorize and simplify the journey that all entrepreneurs, artists, or anyone successful have to take to get there. The way is a roller-coaster ride full of dramatic ups followed by dramatic downs. We spend sleepless nights worrying about cash flow and bills, then celebrate wildly when a big program gets the results we worked so hard for. When the challenges are stripped out of the experience, it leaves little room for the real story of individuals who are trying to make the impossible possible. When there is only celebration of the outcome and little talk of the journey, the path can feel lonely and at times very scary for those on it.

These conversations with friends and colleagues led me to ask if I had lost anything of myself while fulfilling my ambitions in my work. My friend Leo and I talked it over on a long plane ride from New York to Dubai. We were both being celebrated at a major world summit for our successes as young global leaders. Our conversation was the story of searching for our true selves.

Leo was very successful in the business world. He was smart, charismatic, and good-looking, just the kind of guy people trusted.

At twenty years old he had been recruited by Citibank along with two others from a pool of fifteen hundred candidates. The bank saw that he had the right mix of qualities to rise to the top of international finance. They invested in him, giving him scholarships, prestigious internships, and access to exclusive meetings. Leo was on an elite leadership track right from his undergraduate days.

When Leo and his two young colleagues started the high-level jobs they'd been groomed for, the bank chairman wanted to meet them. In preparation, Leo had bought an expensive suit in his favorite color—brown. His style was chic and a bit funky, so he had matching shoes and tie, too. When Leo arrived at the meeting, confident, excited, and looking sharp, the chairman called him over.

"This is the name and address of my tailor," he said giving Leo a card. "Go to him for a new suit. In this business, suits are always blue. Black for evening events. The shirt—always white. Never colored. The shoes—always blue, black, or brown. Your tie can have some color, but don't go wild. The socks always white, blue, brown, or black. No funky colors there. No more of this—" the CEO waved at the stylish suit. "And never brown again. That does not work here."

Leo took the card. He made sure he got himself not one but many blue suits. Over the years, the leadership track paid off. He made lots of money and rose up through the banking world. He also met and married a beautiful woman who was committed to social justice work. When she asked him how he measured success, he thought the answer was money. But he was already making great money—for Citibank, Lehman Brothers, and others—and the work never stopped. He earned more and more, lived a big life, and closed deals all over the world, from Chile to London to Switzerland to New York. He had never actually thought about what his own threshold for success was. How much money did he need to have in order to consider himself successful? How much was enough?

It was many years later, after years of living a very good life, that the light went on for him. His kids were playing in his large walk-in closet in his latest house.

"Daddy, is your favorite color blue?" his daughter asked him.

"I don't know. Why, honey?"

"All of your suits are blue. And your other clothes are blue, too. So it looks like you love blue."

Until then, he had not noticed that all his suits were the same color. Nor did he notice that all his shirts were white, all his shoes were brown or blue or black, and all his ties were conservative except for the one or two that had a red stripe or pink accent. He had followed the formula for success, and it had worked. He could just no longer remember what his own tastes and preferences were.

"Did I wear blue suits because I liked blue? Or because that's what my boss had told me to do?" he said to me. "I could not recall." What part of life was he living out of his true taste or desire, and what part was just because it was *what you did*?

Many of us are like Leo. We project the look or behaviors of success. We jump on the train that our parents, our families, teachers, bosses, and cultures have set for us, and we keep going and going, gathering momentum, waving to the people who admire us and envy us. Yet we rarely pause to ask, "Who am I on this ride?" Or, as Native Americans ask, *When was the last time I danced the dance of my life? When was the last time I sang the song of my life?*

It takes courage to ask these questions. It takes courage to ask if our current path, which has been fruitful and promising, is also compromising us. What is our own definition of success, and are we living by it? How much did our own hearts inform that definition? Where do we stand now? Have we lost our way at all? Think of the lawyer whose sole dream was to be a full-time novelist or the manager who wants to launch a start-up. It can be challenging to listen to and explore what our hearts are telling us. Staying on the familiar path means walking with solid ground under our feet: practicing law or being a manager fulfills our own and other people's expectations. Answering our hearts' call and exploring it is like jumping off the cliff into the unknown.

We are afraid to jump off that cliff, and yet we are also afraid not to jump. Our hearts want to be heard, but the unknown is terrifying. If we jump, will we land safely? Are we courageous enough to free ourselves, no matter what comes next? Or do we stay on that shaky cliff edge instead and suppress the calling inside us?

Nearly two decades after founding Women for Women International and growing it into one of the largest women's rights organization in America, I myself stood on this cliff. I was in my office late one evening, going over spreadsheets and combing through the numbers we needed to make it through the next quarter. Since the organization had grown so much and continued to grow, I often found myself in this position—not out in the field, meeting and helping the people we served, but poring over numbers, going to receptions, meeting donors. I was the face of the organization, and I needed to be everywhere. Yet my true passion had never been fundraising. My passion was to be working directly with women in their countries and individual contexts, hearing their stories and learning from their wisdom as they rebuilt their lives.

This evening I was suddenly overwhelmed by all of it. I felt backed into a corner. I was tired, very tired. I had given the organization everything I had—my passion, my time, my privacy, and everything in my heart and soul. For years and years, I did not take time to have fun or relax. I squeezed out every drop of my soul for the women we were helping and for the organization. I was also a very long way from the uninhibited early days when I had gone wherever I wanted, helping whomever needed it.

I held my head in my hands and started to cry.

Right at that moment my office door swung open, and in rushed my colleague, Erica. She hadn't knocked—she didn't realize that I was still there. She just wanted to drop off a document on my desk.

Seeing my face wet with tears, she stopped in her tracks: "Are you okay?" Erica was in charge of fundraising, so she knew the stress we were under.

"I have created my monster," I cried. The very group that I had founded out of love and a sense of urgency had become my prison. I felt anything but free. Erica gave me an understanding look, then closed the door to allow me privacy.

What I had started as a small personal effort to help women in Bosnia and Herzegovina had become a very major undertaking. I was surrounded by staff, donors, and boards who asked for every moment of my life. No matter how much I gave of myself, there was more and more work to be done and more demands to meet. I was exhausted.

But I didn't know when or how to stop. As the crown of success had descended on my head, so had shackles closed around my feet.

My commitment, ambition, and drive to help women were so strong that I had never taken a moment to step back and ask myself what kind of success would satisfy me. By the time I realized that others thought I was quite successful, I, like Leo, had forgotten myself. My constant and urgent focus on our work blinded me to the questions of "What kind of life did I want to live beyond my work and my cause?" "Who was I outside of my association with my career?" "Who was I inside of it?" I was on a mission to change the world. All I could see was that goal. I could work without stopping to spend time with family or friends. Nothing else was more important—not my health or my well-being. I had no other dream.

Underneath this forward charge was my fear of leadership. I saw leaders in the world causing separation rather than connection, division rather than unity. So many led with arrogance rather than humility and love. Growing up in close proximity to Saddam Hussein had also colored my relationship to leadership and power; to me, those qualities were synonymous with corruption and abuse. So instead of identifying what kind of leadership qualities I admired or wanted to nurture in my role as a CEO, I just saw what I didn't want to become and rejected the whole thing.

The only thing I *did* know from early on was that I would not be one of those people who held on to power no matter what. That didn't happen only to dictators. It happened to business leaders, media moguls, social entrepreneurs, activists, feminists, and humanitarians. Power is power, and humans get attached to power. I vowed that by the time the organization was in good shape, maybe twenty years after we began, I would let go. Other than that one affirmed value, I never thought about what else I was *for* as a leader.

When we operate from a place of fear and rejection, we are in danger of letting others fill in those values for us. We stop owning our process or setting our direction. We stop checking in with our own values. I didn't know that just saying no to what I didn't want without replacing it with any kind of yes made me vulnerable to other people's ideas of what I should do.

My leadership skills didn't keep pace with how Women for Women International grew. We helped thirty-three women in our first year, then one hundred, then one thousand, then a few thousand, and the numbers kept growing into the hundreds of thousands. I was excited that we were making an impact, even if it meant just a smile on one woman's face. It made me believe in the possibilities of change and of dreams coming true. If I, the immigrant to the United States in her early twenties with no work experience and no money, was able to reach so many women and build an organization from scratch, then anyone could do it. It showed me that perseverance could make the impossible possible, even when struggle was part of the process.

But it was hard to face that I was becoming a leader. I didn't want to—I just wanted to get the job done. One day a donor from a foundation visited our offices. I gathered the staff to meet with her, and all of us sat together at an oval-shaped table. I did not pay much attention to where I'd chosen to sit. After the meeting, the donor took me aside.

"You must sit at the head of the table," she said. "That is how you show your leadership."

I had heard so much about how women needed to own their power, how women hesitated to take leadership while their male counterparts jumped into the role, that I said, "Okay," I would do it. That became my habit. When a friend, a donor, or a consultant would suggest that I do something like this, such as sitting at the head of the table, or wearing certain clothes to signal my position, or making sure I had the office of the boss, I would take the advice without thinking. If I had to cultivate the image of a leader, then I supposed I needed all these markers of power and success. I would be fulfilling the role, I thought, even though none of these things mattered that much to me.

It was like I was putting on masks, pretending to be something that I did not identify with in my heart. I was like Leo buying those blue suits. I stepped into the preconceived role of the confident leader, not because it was what I wanted, but because I thought that's what everyone expected from me.

Without a clear sense of myself as the head of the organization, I got confused. I tried to show leadership with my staff, but in truth I came to fear them. I feared that they would judge me if I didn't work harder than

I was asking them to work. I feared overwhelming them with my passion or impatience when they delivered less than what I wanted. I feared imposing unnecessary emotional pressure by talking about the horrors that I was witnessing in the field, so I shared only the less severe stories. I was filtering myself and suppressing my feelings, but my frustration just leaked out around the edges anyway. Everyone felt it. My insecurity was creating pressure on everyone around me as they tried to match the tone and work ethic that I invariably set.

When we lead our lives fearing others, we trigger their fear toward us. It is a vicious cycle that stops only when we lower our walls and show our vulnerabilities authentically instead.

After nearly two decades, I traveled less and less and spent more and more time in front of the computer analyzing spreadsheets. My time was managed by a team that was looking at every inch of my schedule, booking me into one meeting after another, one social event after another, all to raise money. I was a long way from following the flow of my passion—being in the field with the women I existed to serve.

In my work, just like in the late stages of my marriage, my heart was starting to grow silent. The taste of life was going from my mouth. I acted a leader; I did not embrace myself as a leader. I had success in terms of a career and awards, but I did not feel successful inside. I had not allowed myself to stop, reflect, or grow personally. The survival and growth of the organization were utterly consuming, and I justified focusing on them because the need to help more and more women around the world was urgent—and it never ended.

I had been fighting for women's freedom, but I had lost my own freedom. I wanted women to be happy, but I was not happy. I wanted them to be fulfilled in their lives so they could share the best of themselves with their societies, but I was not fulfilled. I had sacrificed myself in the name of serving the cause—but perhaps the cause did not require my sacrifice.

I needed to go back to the source of my passion, to spend time with the women we served. It was my love for them that had driven me to work so hard for so long and that had been the secret of our success as an organization after all. I thought if I could reconnect with them

I could find my happiness again. I decided to make some trips to our offices in various conflict areas, from Afghanistan to Rwanda.

It was my experience meeting Yacuba, an Afghan woman, that led me to the startling awareness that I needed to change my life. She sat in front of me at the Women for Women International office in Kabul telling me her story. Even though it was dramatic, I found myself utterly tired, dragging, as if it was all I could do to listen. She talked of how she had been married off at the age of six to settle a financial debt, how she had felt betrayed by her family but ended up loving the boy they married her to. She consummated her marriage at fifteen and birthed her first baby, with much joy, at sixteen. Then, everything changed. Her family killed her husband, thinking they were freeing her from the marriage. She was furious: first they had abandoned her as a child, then they took away her freedom as a young woman. Her husband had been the family's main provider.

Yacuba stayed living with her very poor in-laws. To survive and raise her daughter, she learned to make hats, selling them on the streets of Kabul. One day, the Taliban accused her of wearing open sandals, which was forbidden for women in public. They whipped her in the street to teach her a lesson. She told me how she felt so humiliated at being beaten in public that she grabbed the arm of the man who was whipping her to stop him. He and the other Taliban members with him were surprised. No woman dared to do that. After few moments of silence, his comrades laughed at him: "A woman stopped you! You deserve it. Now let her go." Yacuba was saved by her courage and a bit of grace.

I had listened to thousands of women sharing their stories of survival, courage, and hope. I had held each one of them in my heart. Yet I found my mind wandering as I listened to Yacuba. *I have heard this story before*, my heart whispered. The story of misery and resilience, of pain and strength, had become so very familiar. I was empty, depleted, and even *bored*.

To catch myself bored in front of the very women I had dedicated my life to was my big act of betrayal—of them and of myself. It was in that moment that I knew I needed to change what I was doing.

It was not easy to articulate that I was no longer happy in my job, that I was resenting the leader I had become, and that I was no longer embodying my own desires in my work. It was confusing because *every* aspect of my life up till then had been about my work. After my encounter with Yacuba, it was obvious that I had lost my equilibrium. I had lost my voice, my individuality, and my joy. I didn't know how to stop—or what to start instead. I just knew that I could not preach the values I could not embody myself. If I really believed in women's freedom to fulfill their full potential, then I could no longer turn my back on my situation by simply working harder. I needed to address it. My silent heart wanted to speak again, wanted its own freedom, even though leaving the safety of my job and comfort of my success would be like jumping off the cliff into the unknown.

A few months after my trip to Kabul, I announced that I was resigning as CEO of Women for Women International. I stood on that cliff, and although the leap looked terrifying, I jumped. It was time to leave what I had built with so much love and passion.

Untangling myself from my organization was like going through a divorce. I had initiated it, but the details of how, when, what to say, and to whom to say it were very painful. Good-byes are never easy for either side, and my stepping down brought up a lot of emotion for everyone. Some colleagues felt abandoned, some were confused, and others were just sad. Still others were happy that I was leaving. It was like the old days when the whole family would go to the airport to bid farewell to a loved one: some relatives would be joking around, while others would be crying; some would be angry and silent, while others would just avoid the whole thing. My team experienced all these feelings. Watching them was difficult, like standing at the center of a tornado. It pulled me this way and that. Throughout, I could hold on to only one thing: I need to hear my heart again.

That space between jumping and landing is where doubt, confusion, fear, and worry rush in. Every leap of faith has this in-between space. I spent the months following my resignation both resting and feeling anxious about the future. Advocating for women's rights was my life's purpose, and that would never change. I was not saying good-bye to the cause, just "See you later." I hoped that in taking this leap of faith I would, in time, know what my heart was calling for. But in the short term, I'd given up the stable life and identity I knew: professional success, financial security, and adventures all over the world. Who was I now? Every time I withdrew money from my account, I'd worry if I'd saved enough to live on until I found my way again. Life was different: Could I pay my bills now that I didn't have a salary? Would I be able to take care of myself?

At social events, simple questions such as "What do you do?" would make me nervous and uncomfortable. At first, I would just say what I'd done for eighteen years: I worked with women survivors of war. If people asked more questions, though, I'd have to admit that actually I was not working at the moment.

When I mustered the courage to say that I wasn't doing much of anything these days, it didn't go well. Nancy, an old friend, was visiting from California and invited me to dinner. When we got to the question of what I was up to, I dared to answer truthfully. "Nothing. I am really doing nothing these days."

Nancy laughed and asked again, "No, really, what are your latest projects?"

People were used to hearing about which country or city I had just been to, or which stories of survival I had witnessed, or what talks I had just given. Neither of us knew what to do when I was no longer sharing my most recent exotic adventure.

"Mostly, I'm knitting, cooking, crying, sleeping, working out, and meditating," I told her. Yes, I was contemplating a new project, but I had nothing specific to report yet. I wasn't sure which one of us was more uncomfortable: me, who for so many years had been charging ahead so fiercely, or her, in not knowing what to make of my true answer.

Our conversation struggled to find another point of connection. We tiptoed around news of common friends, the latest movies, and politics, but we never settled into anything comfortable.

My doubt felt like a green monster sitting on my shoulder constantly whispering in my ear about all the things I should be afraid of. Was I going to land on my feet? Did I want to go back to what I knew and what was safe, ignoring the ache in my heart again? *Was this risk really worth it?*

The choice became either to listen to my green monster or to order it to be silent and instead trust my heart's intelligence. Trusting myself was where I needed true courage. I needed to get quiet in this space of unknowing, even if I was afraid. I didn't know if my wings would spread, if my fears would betray me, or if my sense of purpose would hold me. It was both exhilarating and terrifying at the same time.

Sitting in the silence in the months after my resignation, without the intensity of work to distract me, I started to hear the pulse of my heart in ways I had not before. At first, when I was home alone, pain showed up. Not just the loneliness and doubt about making the leap, but all the feelings I'd suppressed about the rapes and murders, all the hardships and cruelties I'd witnessed all over the world throughout the years. They came pouring out of my body at once. It was staggering.

The process of reacquainting myself with myself changed everything. I learned to be with my feelings instead of fighting them. I would look at sadness and say, "Okay, so this is what sadness feels like." Or, "Oh, there is anger. Now I know. This is impatience." Whenever I brushed aside a negative feeling or difficult memory or resisted it, it got hungrier and more insistent. My resistance exaggerated the feelings' intensity within me, whereas simply allowing them made them pass faster. So I began to allow them to wash over me without panicking or hiding from them. They always left eventually—whether in an hour or in a day or in a week. Once I knew this, each emotion became a book in the library of my life. As I studied and explored it I understood it—and myself—better.

It was painful, yet experiencing these intense feelings gave me the opportunity to know what I actually felt about a lot of things. I got to ask: Was it my staff who had been overbooking me, or did I overcommit? Until I stepped down, I had no idea about these basic things. I discovered that I said more yeses than noes when asked to do things, and I also changed my mind constantly about where and when to meet. It had been me jamming up my schedule all along. I couldn't blame anyone else.

More than anything, my connection to myself allowed for a much deeper level of connection with the people around me. When I could show up authentically in myself, I could show up authentically with others. When I stopped judging all the ways I had failed or fallen short, I stopped judging others' failures, too. It was like being a scientist who was testing the medicine on herself before administering it to others. As I understood each feeling fully, I had a lot more empathy for everyone. I learned to trust my body and to listen to my gut instincts. I surrounded myself with people whose perspectives I trusted, too: peers, mentors, and therapists. From this new place of self-awareness and this new experience of support, I started to discover how I wanted to live, who I wanted to become, and what the new rhythm of life might feel like.

I started taking the same concepts I had been advocating for the world and applying them to myself. If I wanted women to be happy and free to express themselves fully, then I needed to be happy and free to express my heart's desires. If I was advocating for kindness toward others, I needed to understand the meaning of kindness toward myself. If I wanted people to be courageous and stand against injustice, I needed to have the courage to speak my truth in the simplest contexts, whether that was in a work meeting or in a family gathering, with staff, in my circle of friends, or in myself. It took courage to overcome fear, to go within, and to speak up. But I no longer wanted to walk on eggshells with anyone; I never wanted to hide who I was or raise a wall of fear again when I feared others.

All I could do was be truthful in my aspirations and needs, my hopes, fears, and vulnerabilities. I needed to be myself out in the open, knowing fully that there would be times when I would overwhelm people or be too direct or too impatient. Now, I could also be aware of my behavior and its impact, and stay open to other people's reactions to it. Rather than hiding, fearing, or resenting a criticism, I could hear it and own it, if it was true, without panicking. "Oh, yes, I know I am impatient," I could say. "Thank you for reminding me of that."

Leo, my banker friend, eventually left his job in the world of finance to run other businesses. He has discovered that his favorite color really is blue, not because it's the color of financial success but because he actually likes it. His definition of success has changed, thanks to his children's observation and his wife's support. Now, only making money is no longer enough for him. He makes sure that whatever venture he's involved in gives back to the world environmentally and socially, that it integrates social benefits with financial benefits.

He has started a reforestation project and has founded a company whose profits in part help marginalized youth with their education and careers. Along the way, he tells his teams and the people he serves to make sure they define what success is to them. He asks them how they will know, for themselves, when they've "made it." He makes a lot less money now, but his life and work are much richer in other ways. His goal has changed to having a full life rather than only full financial success.

I stayed on the board of Women for Women International for two more years after I stepped down to support the transition to a new leadership. I left at exactly the twentieth anniversary of the organization, just as I had promised myself I would when I was twenty-three years old. In those two years, I realized my next goal. I wanted to discover the "secret sauce" that would lead to lasting change in women's lives. It was a question we were always trying to answer at Women for Women International. I had every confidence that we'd done a lot of good in the world, but the issues could seem insurmountable. In one of my last field trips, I'd asked Seida, a Bosnian colleague, this question.

"Zainab, the answer is simple," she said, holding my hand. "The secret sauce to helping women is inspiration. All we need is to show women there is hope and a way out of their oppression and sadness. Everything else, every program, every action is just a tool for helping them find the courage to change their lives."

My next goal would be to inspire women by featuring their stories through media projects in the Middle East and in the United States. I would begin with a TV show for Arab and Muslim women to acknowledge their voices and show them the possibilities of change from within their cultures and religions. It was a way to build small bridges between women in the same regions rather than only building big bridges between women in different cultures and continents.

I was excited about my new initiative, but in the lead-up to the launch, I felt some lingering fear of leadership. I knew I needed to address it, but I didn't quite understand what I was still resisting.

A conversation with a mentor showed me the way. I went to her for guidance on my new show, which was partly inspired by her show in America. In the midst of our talk I started crying out of worry and fear for this new journey I was embarking on. She asked what I was afraid of.

"I am afraid of leadership." I explained my past experiences, how I had resisted the role, left it undefined, and how that hadn't worked. I left our meeting that afternoon with a new realization inspired by her wisdom: I needed to own my leadership, to embody my own values in every step, every action, and every decision I made as a leader. If I let others define leadership for me, I would continue to resent and fear it. When we lead out of the desire to please, no matter how much we try, it will never be good enough. We can never fulfill other people's expectations or dreams of who we should be. We can be true only to our authentic voice, even if that is different from what the world tells you it should be.

I suddenly realized that here, too, I needed to be authentic. Leadership, like everything else, had to be heartfelt. When it was about the heart rather than the mask I felt I had to wear, it would not be a burden at all.

After that conversation, I could appreciate my own leadership for the first time. I had always followed my gut instincts. I could tolerate risk and stay in the place of unknowing until things clarified and I knew what to do. These were great strengths that allowed me to get through the uncertain roller-coaster moments of my life. Realizing this put me at ease. I could step back, look inward, and acknowledge that I *was* a leader, in my own way and with my own values.

Then the concepts of leadership and success became calmer and humbler. They lost the grandiose and even fearful meaning they once had in my life. When we are transparent about ourselves and our values, leadership becomes a walk of clarity, humility, and self-awareness. Giving and receiving are no longer fraught or exhausting. We do not have to shut out our hearts so that we can focus on our mission or ambitions, nor do we have to sacrifice our health and well-being to do good in the world. Everything becomes an expression of our authentic selves.

Today, I am as proud of leaving Women for Women International as I am of founding it. Building an organization is one thing. Willingly letting go of power is another thing altogether. In the letting go, I was walking my own truth and experiencing how it feels to listen to my heart, to allow for change, to take a huge risk and understand all that means. I knew intimately how it felt to jump off that cliff not knowing how or when I'd land—just trusting that I would.

To be a leader and acknowledge that we've truly succeeded is the same as being a full human: we need to be exactly ourselves, in our truth. That's when we can give our best. In our authenticity we can dare to break the generally accepted rules and to make new ones that better suit who we are. Those who resist this creative engagement are simply afraid. Our work is to not make their fears ours—instead, we need to make our freedom theirs. That is when we can jump with full confidence that our wings will open and we will land safely, wherever and however we land.

4

Making Amends

We can see our full selves
only when we acknowledge both the
light and the shadow within us.

e all have done something in our lives that we are embarrassed to acknowledge out loud. We are afraid that we won't be loved or accepted if we disclose the things that, deep in our hearts, we are not proud of—the times we stereotyped or belittled another person, cheated them or mocked them. It's hard to make amends for times when we used another person or witnessed an injustice but did nothing about it. It's easier to point the finger at all the larger wrongs that are happening in the world and say, "The real problem is out there—those guys are doing such terrible things; those guys are the monsters."

We can deny our little personal wrongs for as long as we want. They are easy to deny. It's much harder to fully admit to ourselves that we are in denial. Yet, if we listen, the whispers of our secrets never go away. They are like annoying mosquitoes on a hot summer night: no matter how much repellent we use, they still find some exposed patch of skin. Denying that we are culpable chips away at our credibility, too. By claiming that we are living righteous lives free of wrongdoing when really we are just hiding our trespasses, we undermine our own integrity. We think that by standing in the sun, no one will see our shadow. Unfortunately, our shadow is always seen. It was a brothel owner in Delhi, India, who taught me this.

When I was asked by CNN to do a piece for the Freedom Project as part of a series they were producing on trafficking of women and children, I was excited. This story was exactly in my wheelhouse. I called my friend Ruchira Gupta, founder of Apne Aap Women Worldwide, an organization that helps trafficked women in India who have been prostituted. I asked her to help connect me to a brothel owner who would be willing to talk to me about how trafficking works. Ruchira was often in the red light district of New Delhi helping women get new skills and education so they could leave sex work, with all its abuses, behind. Part of the problem prostituted women face is a lack of income; outside of the red light district, the stamp of dishonor is branded on them, reducing their options for earning a living.

Ruchira was able to arrange a rare meeting for me with Hassan, a brothel owner. He agreed to speak with me on the condition that I film him with the brothel's sewing studio in the background. Hassan prided himself on being different than other brothel owners. He didn't just turn out older women when they had become less attractive to his clients. He gave them and their children shelter and taught them new skills so that they could earn money while still living under his roof.

I went to meet him in the afternoon, a slow time in the red light district. Women and girls were washing their clothes or decorating themselves with bright makeup in preparation for evening customers. Everyone peeked at me and my crew from balconies or behind windows and doorways. All eyes were on us as we walked through the colorful streets with murals and posters of actresses, overlaid with tangles of electric wires. I was obviously a foreigner and not from the district, plus I was being followed by a camera and a sound man, so we really stood out. The red light district is not an easy place to be when you don't know the rules. It is an underworld of its own, with laws that we couldn't know about nor protections for us if we broke them.

When we reached the brothel, an older woman opened the door, showed us to Hassan's office, and offered us tea. She was one of the "retired" prostitutes. Hassan arrived half an hour later, and immediately it was clear that he was the king of his business. He was a small man, almost petite, with a strong voice, a strong handshake, and a forceful demeanor. His hands were covered in gold rings to show his wealth and power. His cell phone never stopped ringing. We sat facing each other for the interview, but at an unusually long distance so that the camera could get shots from several angles. It was an emotional distance, too: we came from almost diametrically opposed worlds. He exploited and oppressed women, and I fought for their rights and freedom.

Hassan was very matter-of-fact about his business. He described how he bought women and girls, sometimes as young as eleven years old, from pimps and madams who trafficked them. Most of the girls and women were very vulnerable, coming from situations of violence, abuse, or poverty. With few options to support or protect themselves, they fell into traffickers' hands. Hassan would assess each one to decide if he wanted her. If he did, he would negotiate the arrangement in front of her, even though she had no choice in the matter.

"I tell her, 'I am buying you for this amount. You have to pay me back by working for free for five years. Then you can leave.'" During those five years, the girl or woman had to sleep with between five and fifteen men a day. Hassan paid for her food and shelter but deducted these costs from her earnings, prolonging her debt to him. If she had a child from one of the customers, he sent the child to school, but added those costs to the mother's debt. He portrayed his system as taking care of the women and their children, but in reality he made it hard for them to get out of debt and actually earn their freedom.

Hassan was clear about his work. He knew how vulnerable the girls and women were, and he knew how to make money from their vulnerability. He had no ambivalence at all and no remorse; he was a businessman. In fact, he saw himself as providing safety and jobs for women who otherwise would be living on the streets. I listened to him with open curiosity. I really wanted to know how things worked, even as I saw his business model as a form of enslavement.

As our conversation continued, Hassan was not content to just be the subject of our interview. He wanted to tell *me* something, too. He wanted to talk about all of us and how our collective actions and attitudes toward these women seal their fate.

"You laugh at the jokes about prostitutes," he said. His stare was piercing. "You judge these women for being immoral, but you do not see how you are part of the system they are trapped in. You make jokes about them and laugh at them. You imprison them for being prostitutes. You do not see that it is your sons, your brothers, your fathers, and your husbands who create the market for someone like me to take advantage of. As women, you mistreat your servants, pay them too little, and kick them out when you don't like their work. What do you think happens to these women then? Who do you think comes to the rescue when you force them out? I do. I make them work for me, but I also provide them with shelter. You think you are on a higher moral ground. But you are part of what makes the red light district possible."

He had turned the tables on me. Even as a women's rights activist, I had never thought about this. He was right. I *had* thought of them as immoral women. I had been at those dinners where people told jokes involving prostitutes. I, too, had joined in the laughter without much thought for the reality of these women's lives, the circumstances that had landed them in prostitution. Until that point, it never occurred to me that the men I was sitting with—friends, families, acquaintances—may have used prostitutes, even as they made jokes at their expense.

Hassan knew all of these inconsistencies. He knew about men who claimed to be upstanding but secretly bought sex from women ensnared in a system that abused and despised them. He knew all about the women who claimed to be educated and aware yet treated their maids and servants badly. He knew how everyone mocked prostitutes yet also exploited them. Those in the red light district were aware about who they were. It was a blind spot only for me and people like me, who lived outside of the red light district. Even if we refused to see our role in it, we were implicated.

We were all part of the problem, no matter what our social status was, our education level or our wealth or nationality. As long as we denied this, pretending that we didn't have anything to do with the red light district, Hassan felt justified in his work. I left our interview that day understanding this. While I didn't agree that his business was benign, as he tried to portray it, he had a point: it was time for me to own my part of the story and not simply point my finger at him alone as a horrible man who enslaved all these women. It was time to have uncomfortable conversations with men in my life. It was time to ask them what had never occurred to me to ask before: had they ever paid for sex?

I'd thought that men who used prostitutes were "those other men," not the men in my own family or circle of friends, acquaintances, and colleagues—all of whom I considered educated, enlightened, and refined. Now, I needed to know the truth. In my experience, to get truthful answers I have to ask the question with genuine curiosity, without preconceived ideas or judgments. It was the only way honest conversations could happen. In fact, that's how I'd approached the brothel owner as well.

With this attitude, I asked the men in my life, "Have you ever been to a prostitute?" Some men said they had never paid for sex. But, to my surprise, a lot of men said yes. Many told me that their first sexual experience was with a prostitute. Others told me how they had taken their teenage sons to prostitutes to introduce them to sex, or hired women during their travels, or had been offered prostitutes during their work dealings, and so on. Some even brought prostitutes to their homes when their wives were out of town. Some were uncomfortable with the experience and never did it again. Some had no remorse and continued to do it. But all around me were men who paid for sex, and *none* of them had ever stopped to think about how their actions might be connected to human trafficking or might contribute to the abuse these women faced.

Some of us have the luxury of hiding behind nice clothes, good education, and elegant talk. Privilege protects privilege (and, conversely, poverty leads to more vulnerability). Why talk about how we have used other human beings when we're just trying to get ahead in a tough world? Why admit to some small vice or minor exploitation that no one seems to care about and that we do not want to give up?

The more stature we have, the more attached we are to losing that status. If we take responsibility for our actions and inactions in our past, we fear losing all we have worked for or have gotten used to enjoying. How many women suspect that the men close to them go to prostitutes but look the other way rather than risk starting a fight or shaking up the family? How aware are we of our own culpability toward the women in our own red light districts, whether they are literal or metaphorical? Do we further the vulnerability of others without even thinking about it—without wanting to think about it?

I had often avoided pointing out uncomfortable truths so as not to be the boring or annoying person at a party or in a social setting. But now it *was* my turn to look at my own uncomfortable truths. I could no longer turn away. While I had never paid for sex, I had to ask myself what I had done in my life that might have hurt another person or caused an injustice, whether in big or small ways, without me realizing it. Whatever it was, I needed to deal with it and make amends.

I told my activist friend Penny that I needed to acknowledge these shadows in my life and deal with the things I was not proud of. She was perplexed.

"Why bother exploring your small wrongdoings when there are so many big wrongs in the world that we need to fight against?" she asked. "You are fighting for women's rights all over the world—that's already so much more than what many people do. Why dig into the not-so-great actions of your past? Whatever they are, they cannot be as bad as the damage that racists, sexists, and bigots are doing."

Penny had a point. Human rights issues are big, and they are urgent. Yet her argument was focused only on the short term. If we want to create more permanent changes in these big issues, our actions have to come from the core of our integrity, not from our righteousness. To live in integrity, we need to look inward and deal with things in ourselves that we have not wanted to confront. Whether big or small, we all have something that weighs on us. Owning up to our transgressions is the only way we can free ourselves from the shame that haunts our hearts—the shame we have even when no one else can see it. When we fight for the bigger issues in the world from a full awareness of ourselves in *both* our light and our shadow, our calls to action have full integrity.

It's easy to worry that coming clean will mean destroying everything that we have built or hurt everyone we love. But coming clean does not always lead to hurt. If the approach is sincere, our efforts to make amends have a chance of doing more good than harm. Acknowledging our actions and missteps is needed at the very least in the privacy of our lives, in our hearts, or with those we most trust. We can own our vulnerabilities and still be kind to ourselves. If we look directly at where we're out of integrity, speak to it, address it, work on it, we come out the other side stronger. That's where we find freedom in ourselves and also freedom from the likes of the brothel owner who sees our shadow so clearly, calls it out, and uses it to justify his own actions.

My personal story of shame was not related to a big story out in the world. It was not related to any financial, sexual, or moral corruption. It was not an *issue* that needed to be tackled. It was a cruelty that I had showed to a vulnerable girl when I was a child. The hurt I had caused was a small thing. It happened one afternoon and passed in a couple of hours, but it had weighed on me for my whole life. I had never properly acknowledged it and never been able to make amends. It whispered to me, *But, Zainab, you did that*—and I would hush these whispers, but they never died. So the story came back over and over again; it had its own life within me and carried its own pain. Looking it in the eyes, addressing it, and releasing it was key to my freedom and growth.

My story of reconciliation started when I was going to an exclusive private reception for women's rights leaders at the State Department with Hillary Clinton, who was then secretary of state. It was the peak of my career. I was in the back of a taxi in Washington, DC, and we were stuck in traffic. Absentmindedly, I checked my email and saw a new message from George, a young Iraqi staff member at Women for Women International's office in Baghdad. The subject line said: "Is this you?"

In the message was a picture of myself at fourteen years old, lying sick in bed with Radya, our family maid, who was only two years older than me. I was wearing my blue pajamas, and my hair was big and bushy. And there was Radya, with her chocolate-brown skin, her beautiful dimples, sitting next to me with her messy hair and straight white teeth, wearing the shabby dress she wore when cleaning the house.

I stared at the picture. I had not seen Radya in twenty years, even though we'd grown up together in my parents' household. Radya had been our family's child maid. As we'd grown older, she had become the keeper of my secrets and the witness of my life. I had not had any news about her since I'd come to America, even though I had asked around and tried to find out what had happened to her. For all these years, a secret shame had been buzzing and whispering in my brain about her. I had an apology to make.

I quickly wrote back to George. "Yes! That is me. Where did you get this picture from?"

He responded by forwarding the email that Radya had sent to her Women for Women International sponsor, a woman named Suzanne. Sponsors sent not only thirty dollars a month to women survivors of war but letters and pictures, too. This helped to create a far bigger connection and emotional link than just sending money ever could. After helping hundreds of thousands of women, this program I'd designed also connected me to the woman I had been hoping to find again one day.

Dear Suzanne,

My name is Radya Jarad. I have six children, four girls and two boys. We were displaced from Baghdad when my husband was killed by terrorists. I grew up since childhood in a very poor family. My father was a guard in Baghdad and we lived wherever he worked. I was eight years old when a very gracious family adopted us. My mother had worked for the family before I did, but they did not make me feel that I was the daughter of their housekeeper. The family had their own daughter. I loved her more than myself. I wore her clothes and slept in her bed. We ate together and played together. We have been separated since we grew up and I have been looking for her. She saved me in childhood. I am happy now because I found another sister in you. Thank you for this support. I will send you my picture with my old childhood friend, my sister. I have nothing of her but her photographs and some of her clothes, which she gave me and I kept.

Me and Zainab Tariq Rashid were sisters from childhood and I lived in sorrow when I lost her.

In peace,
Radya

She was referring to my father's and grandfather's last name, Rashid, rather than my family's name, Salbi. "This is indeed me," I responded to George. "Do you know if she has heard my name in connection to Women for Women International?" He said she didn't know anything.

"Okay, please do not tell her about me. I am going to come to Iraq to visit her, and I want it to be a surprise. Make sure she is okay until I get there and can take care of things myself. I know this woman. She is part of my life."

At the prestigious State Department gathering, among top women leaders in America, all I could think of was Radya. Her letter had brought my past directly into my present. She had been ten years old when she came to live with us, and I had been eight. Radya's father had been a guard, and her mother had been a maid. They had six children and needed Radya to work to pay for her eldest brother's education. In our household, she, the poor one, and I, the well-off one, had both been my mother's daughters. No matter how hard I tried to be present during the reception that evening, my heart and mind were back in my childhood, back home in Baghdad with my lost sister.

It took me five months to get back to Iraq. In Baghdad I picked up my Iraqi colleague, George, and my cousin, Ahmed, who wanted to join us, and we drove two hours south of Baghdad to an internally displaced person's camp in the province of Karbala. The drive went through miles and miles of desert, through security checkpoints, past orange orchards shaded by palm trees, past many small villages settled on the edge of the Tigris River. As we entered Karbala, a religiously conservative city in central Iraq, I covered my jeans and T-shirt—normal city clothes in Baghdad—with an *abya*, a long piece of black linen that draped me from head to toe.

The dirt roads to the internally displaced people's camp were full of open sewers, dirty water, and garbage. It was not a formal government area but an informal collection of mud homes built randomly as each person or family took refuge from wherever they were escaping. We stopped at the Women for Women International office to pick up Amal, the organizer and trainer who had been overseeing Radya's case locally. Amal had been visiting Radya and her children regularly to make sure they were doing well until I could get there.

Amal showed us the way to Radya. She was our guide to the camp and our introduction to Radya. We were obviously out of place. People could see from the way we walked, talked, and dressed—even how I wore the abya—that we were from the capital city.

When we arrived at Radya's simple mud home, it was Amal who knocked on the door, while the rest of us stood back. *Amal* means "hope" in Arabic. As she knocked, saying, "It's me—Amal, Amal," I thought, *Hope is knocking on Radya's door.* Hope that we could be reunited. Hope that in reconnecting we could help her out of whatever she had gone through—out of displacement, poverty, hopelessness.

Radya opened her door, also wearing an abya, except hers was full of dust. She wore it as if she never took it off. I stood in front of her, but her look of wonder made it clear that she didn't recognize me. There was part of me that didn't recognize her, either. "I am Zainab," I said. She shook her head as if to say she didn't know this Zainab.

"I am Zainab," I repeated.

After a few seconds, a look of shock and disbelief crossed her face. "Zainab. *Zainab?* Zainab, the daughter of Umm Zainab?" In Iraq, people call a mother by the relationship to her first child.

I confirmed, yes, it was me. She stepped forward. "Oh, Zainab! Oh Zainab! If you only knew what has happened to me!"

Radya embraced me, weeping and moaning. I tried to speak but was overcome by emotion myself. *I've found her at last*, I thought, *this girl—this woman—who had been part of my family for so long, whom I had loved and missed so much.* Radya, whom I had been searching for and with whom I needed to make amends.

She took my hands and led me into her home. It was just two mud rooms with a straw carpet and mattresses piled to the side, not so different from the ones she'd grown up in. She had changed a lot in twenty years. I recognized the dimple in her cheek, but she had gained weight and carried herself differently from the young woman of twenty-three whom I last saw in 1990. I still had doubts that I was talking to the right woman. I took her left hand and pushed up her sleeves to see the burn marks I remembered. She had burned herself as a child while baking bread in a traditional Iraqi mud oven. They were there. She smiled and asked me if I still had the birthmarks on my stomach. Yes, yes, I assured her. Those marks are almost entirely faded now; only someone who'd known me as a child could know that I once had them. Then she jumped up to the only cabinet in the empty room and took down a teapot, marble eggs, and an old photo album that she had kept from the days when she lived with my family. "I have very little from the past," she said. "I had to run from Baghdad after the militias killed my husband. In the rush, I only managed to take what was most important to me. Do you remember these things that you gave me when we were children?"

She was indeed my Radya.

Her four daughters and two sons were too shy to meet me and my team, so they hid in the other room as she told me about her life.

"It was the Sunni-Shia fighting that killed my husband. He owned an electronics store, and we had been doing well. We had built our home together and were very happy as a family. Two men came into his shop one afternoon and shot him in the head—because he was a Shia. I was terrified that they would come to kill me and my children, too. Less than two weeks later, I packed everything I could carry in a pickup truck and came here to the internally displaced people's camp. I left my home that we'd built brick by brick. Just left it! It was safer for us in Karbala. But I had no income, no protection, and six kids to feed. Some family members promised to help us—my husband's brothers and other men in the family—but none of them ever showed up. I was left alone to fend for my children. That was four years ago. Ever since, I have experienced utter poverty. I have seen the worst, Zainab. I have been hungry, with no food to feed my children. It is truly a miracle that we are still alive."

Radya explained how she carried her husband's gun and stayed awake all night to protect her children from any attacks in the camp. She had lived at times on only bread and tomatoes, and had gone days with no water.

"I have seen the worst, Zainab. I have called for you so many times in my heart. I can't believe you found me." At these words, we hugged and cried.

There was so much more to talk about. But first I needed to attend to the essentials. I needed to make sure that her family was taken care of. We had to figure out how to get her a regular monthly income. She needed better housing, her kids needed help with school, and they all needed more meat and other protein to eat. I was happy to learn that one of her daughters was studying business administration in college, another was studying nursing, and another was preparing to go into pharmaceutical studies. I was shocked that she had also married her girls off at fifteen or sixteen, but when she explained that she did it to make sure they would have the security to continue their education, I understood. She was doing what she had to do to protect her daughters; she had made their education a condition of the marriages. It's easy to see her actions as backward if one doesn't take into account the circumstances she faced. I could not judge her choices even if I was generally against girls marrying so young.

When her immediate well-being was taken care of, I asked Radya if she wanted to come visit me at my uncle's home so we could take our time catching up. She agreed. A few days later we met in Baghdad at my Uncle Fouad's house on the Tigris River where she, too, had spent a lot of her childhood.

When Radya arrived, my aunt, uncle, and cousins showered her with hugs and kisses, and we all drank lots of tea, brewed in the traditional Iraqi way with cardamom, and ate sliced fruit and palm dates. We sat in rooms where the walls were not mud at all, like in Radya's home, but sturdy brick decorated with Persian carpets, crystal lights, and paintings of semi-naked dancing women. The house still had the lush garden full of blossoming roses, gardenias, and jasmine where we had played as children. I had swum in the pool there with my cousins while Radya had looked on in case I needed help.

Everyone in my family had wondered what had happened to Radya during the invasions and the militia fighting, but no one had known where to find her. In the midst of sectarian violence, families in Baghdad had become isolated within their individual neighborhoods. This had happened to Radya, as it had happened to millions of other Iraqis.

After tea, Radya and I excused ourselves from the family gathering to catch up privately. There was so much to talk about. Our lives had changed, and so had we. We sat in a beautiful living room on the second floor, making ourselves comfortable on the white sofa, under paintings of Arabian horses. From where we sat, we could look out over the Tigris. When Radya took off her head scarf, I saw that her hair still had a pretty curl to it. She took off her shoes, too, and spread out on the sofa, sighing with relief. I took her feet in my hands to massage them as we talked about how we used to hang out in this same room as children.

Going over the memories of our childhood, we giggled like two young girls. We had both married as very young women twenty years earlier. I had lived vicariously through her stories of love letters and secret meetings as she'd been falling in love with Sabar, her brother's friend. I'd wanted to know all about their hushed plans to save up and get married. She knew that I had left for an arranged marriage in America. Just as we started to talk, there was a knock on the door, and the new maid, a woman from Indonesia—who had left three children behind to work in Baghdad—came in offering us coffee and dates, fruits and biscuits. We grew quiet as the new maid served me and the former maid.

I looked at Radya. Now was the moment. "I don't think I have ever apologized to you for how I hurt you when we were children," I said. Radya immediately knew what I was talking about. She remembered that day, too. It had been a turning point in our relationship.

The day Radya moved in, my mother explained why her parents had sent her to work for us. The extra income would help her family. Her father had guarded our family's home when we went on vacation, and her mother used to clean for us. Now they had bought some land outside of the city, I was to treat Radya as part of the family.

"Now you have a sister," she said.

A sister? I didn't want a sister. I was content being the only girl who got all of her parents' attention. So, at first, I ignored Radya.

I was consumed in my own world, doing my homework and playing with my friends, my Barbie dolls, and all the other childhood games I loved. Like most live-in maids, Radya existed in the shadows, like a ghost. I never saw her. I didn't know where she slept, where she kept her clothes, or how she liked to spend her free time. Radya was there to serve me and my family. That was all she meant to me.

My indifference was harsh, but it was a fact. Then one afternoon I came home from school and wanted a treat. I was in first grade.

My mom was still at work, and my father was on one of his trips, so it was just me and my baby brother in the house with Radya. I was still in my school uniform, a blue skirt and white shirt, and Radya was wearing the dress she wore for cleaning, busily preparing lunch for the family.

"I want to eat coconut ice cream," I told Radya in my most commanding voice.

"No, you can't. You have to wait for your mother. Eat lunch and then ice cream," she replied. I didn't want to hear this.

"I want to eat the ice cream now, before lunch."

"No, you can't. I will not give it to you. You have to wait until lunch." We continued this way until I lost my temper.

"You're just the maid. It is your job to do as I wish!" My voice was so sharp and so cold that even I was taken aback.

Radya's face crumpled, and her eyes shone with tears. Her bottom lip quivered as she shouted with a trembling voice, "I am not your slave!"

She ran out of the house and off down the street, slamming the front door behind her. I waited in shock for her return. After half an hour or so, when she didn't come back, I panicked. I went searching for her, but I couldn't see her anywhere. I went to sit in the kitchen, feeling sick with fear. I knew my mother would be angry if she found out that I had caused Radya to run away.

When my mother came home, she asked where Radya was. "I don't know," I lied. "She just left."

My mom didn't buy it. She insisted on knowing what had happened. So I told her a milder version of the story.

"She overreacted," I told my mom, as if I couldn't understand what had upset her so much.

My mother rushed out of the house. An hour or so later, she came home with Radya. She had gone to relatives who lived nearby. As soon as I saw my mama's face, I realized she knew the whole story. Oh, she was mad!

It was easy to tell when my mother got angry. Her eyes grew bigger, until they were almost completely round, and small drops of sweat beaded on her upper lip. She didn't scream or shout or do anything dramatic. She took me aside, pinned my shoulders to the wall, and glared at me with her sharp, penetrating eyes.

"What you did was cruel. Very cruel." Her words were short and sharp, and they cut through me. "Never, ever do that to anybody, ever again. Do you understand me?"

Her eyes were so full of anger that they seemed to pierce through to my spine. She did not need to explain anything more.

"You are to apologize to her," my mother ordered. I did apologize. After that, my parents gave me a few household chores to do, and over time my relationship and attitude toward Radya changed. I started allowing her to play with me, and eventually I started paying attention to her. Until then, I had been like one of Cinderella's mean stepsisters. That moment gave me a glimpse of my own insensitivity toward someone less fortunate than me. Although over the years I ended up dedicating my life to serving the poorest of the poor, that childhood experience of my own cruelty never left me.

Radya remembered that moment clearly, too: "It felt like we were the exact opposite of each other. Your parents gave you everything you wanted, while my parents sent me to work. I really hated you for that."

Radya talked and talked about her feelings, ones that I had never heard before. I had thought that we were each other's confidantes as we grew older. But it seemed that she had much more to say than I had ever known. She was animated and direct as she spoke.

"There was one chore I really hated, Zainab—making your bed! No matter how hard I tried to get you to do it yourself in the morning, you never would. And I couldn't stand it when you tried to bake! Every time you made a cake you would make a huge mess, breaking eggs and getting flour everywhere. And I was the one who had to clean up after you. Of course I resented that. Why should I have to clean after you while you got to go to school? You were very spoiled. Your parents threw you the best birthday parties. I enjoyed them, but I also knew that no one would ever throw such a party for me. And you were always talking about your holidays to Los Angeles and Greece. It made me so angry.

"It was your mother who made me feel comfortable and loved. She was so kind and generous to me. She gave me everything: not just material things, but so much love. She would hug me and kiss me and tell me that I was her daughter. I can still remember her sweet smell."

I had no idea that Radya felt hurt beyond that day of my cruelty. She was describing a reality I had not even considered. I had not known what it meant to be the unseen one who was left behind at home as I played and pursued my dreams and studies. She had been the ghost of the house who cleaned up the mess that we had left behind.

I had never thought about life from a maid's perspective, about the fact that I never had to make my bed or that my laundry was done for me. When I was growing up, my mother insisted that I never learn how to cook or clean so that no man could expect me to do these chores just because I was a woman. I had gladly followed her orders and later thought of it as a feminist upbringing. My mother was very passionate about teaching me to be a strong and independent woman. I had incorporated these values in speeches I gave about women's rights all over the world, thinking it was a progressive message.

In truth, it never occurred to me that this story might have an uncomfortable underbelly. My mother had neglected to mention that for women like me to be freed from these chores, someone else had to do the cooking and the cleaning. And it would probably be another woman, most likely a poor woman who didn't have a choice, like Radya. As I listened to Radya's memories of our childhoods, I saw my mother's teachings in a new light. They seemed a lot less enlightened from Radya's perspective.

"I am so sorry, Radya," I said. "I am so, so sorry not only for my cruelty that day. I am sorry for not paying attention to how you felt over those years."

We hugged and cried. Radya had more to say. She continued to speak assertively but without anger. She told her story with a certain force that I had never heard from her before.

"All my six siblings were sent to school, but I was sacrificed. I worked so that my brothers could live their lives. When I asked my father why he didn't send me to school, he told me, 'You are a girl. What would you do with school? I can barely afford to care for this family. You need to help me survive and care for your siblings.' I can still feel the sadness of seeing other girls allowed to enter a world that was forever closed to me. I dreamt of wearing a uniform like them, carrying my books to school like them, and doing homework like them, but I never spoke about my dream with anybody.

"Over time I sat with you, Zainab, as you did homework. I couldn't read or write, but I would ask you about letters and words, and you would explain. That's how I learned. I would be sweeping the floor, listening hard to the words you were repeating, saying them under my breath as you said them out loud. I was so eager to learn, sometimes I even memorized the passages before you did. When the government passed a law saying that all children must go to school, your parents sent me to an evening class close to your home. I was so excited, Zainab, just to get my own schoolbag and fill it with the pencils and erasers and notebooks the government gave us. I didn't mind that I was going in the evening so I could clean the house during the day or that I was the only child among many adult women. I got the highest marks!"

Radya eventually stopped working for my family, finished her education, and took a part-time job at the country club my family went to. Then, she worked as a receptionist at the airport where my dad worked. She never stopped being part of the family, visiting often and frequently spending the night. When she married and Sabar's electronics shop did well, her fortunes rose even more. It was a beautiful story to hear. Then, Sabar's death sixteen years later sent her life tumbling all the way back to ground zero, right back into the desperate poverty of her childhood that she'd worked so hard to escape.

That night, Radya enjoyed a hot bath at my uncle's house. She had not been able to take one for years since her displacement. While she was bathing, my family and I sat in the living room discussing our moral obligations toward her. It was not a straightforward discussion. Some joined me in feeling that we had a duty to help Radya for working as a child servant, and others felt that she had been paid a fair salary back then, so although we should help her out, we didn't have anything to make up for. My brothers and I, who'd had the closest relationships with her, made the final decision. We would give Radya some of the inheritance our mother had left us to support her until her life was back in good shape and her kids were all adults with stable lives.

With some help, Radya moved into a new home in Karbala and got her job back from the same ministry that had hired her when she worked at the airport. Her three daughters finished their nursing, management, and pharmacy studies, two children dropped out of school, and one is still in high school as of this writing. I speak with her regularly now, as a true friend and a sister of the heart.

Our hidden shames never die. We can choose to hold on to them and try to keep them hidden, or we can look at them directly, address them, resolve them, and grow out of them. The choice is ours. When we hold on to them, they haunt us, imprisoning us in their whispers. When we agree to release them, we have to face ourselves. I was lucky to find Radya and be given the chance to acknowledge my actions of the past and make amends for them directly with her. I did it for her, but more than anything, I did it for myself. I needed to release myself from the weight of guilt and shame that haunted me. Making amends to those we have hurt in our lives is a constant process. No matter how much awareness we have, we all make mistakes that hurt others. Making amends is not over when one situation is resolved. Rather, it starts with the first gesture and continues on from there. Mine started with finding Radya.

Sometimes I think I had to go around the world and work with thousands of women trying to escape violence and poverty only to find the very woman I was looking for all along—the one I owed my deepest apology to. In making amends with Radya, I learned of emotions and realities I had never considered before. I would never have otherwise been aware of what it meant to be the one who existed in the shadows, cleaning the mess of my family's life, suffering my insensitivities, and living always with that degree of hurt.

People in the shadows of our lives hold secrets for us. It is up to each one of us to bring that shadow to light. In that is our learning. It matters less how big or small the act is; it matters more how it feels inside our hearts. It's where our conscience hurts that we need to pay attention. I knew this was my story of shame, and it took me a lifetime to face it and own it. In doing so, a deeper awareness arrived in my life. I realized that making amends was a kind of freedom, and so I resolved to continue to practice it. And if I ever see that brothel owner again, I can tell him, "Yes, I know my shame, and I have addressed it. You may never again use it to justify yours."

5

Going Into Our Darkness

When we lead with anger, we risk
becoming the very thing we despise.

Truth is like the story of King Arthur's sword. In the legend, only
the sword's rightful owner, the true heir to the kingdom, can pull
it from the stone in which it is embedded. This idea applies to all
of us as well: to be the full king or queen of the kingdom of our lives,
we too need to claim our own sword of truth.

Every single person can hold his sword and sit on his throne. Everyone can embody her power and rule the kingdom of her life. But we can
do this *only* when we are brave enough to face every aspect of ourselves.
A bully who brags about his power, his physical strength, and his sharp
words will succeed in claiming his sword of truth only when he also
admits to his fears and his feelings of inadequacy and insecurity. To truly
hold her sword, a compulsive flirt who takes pleasure in the attention
she gets would have to acknowledge her pain, insecurities, and need for
love as well. Truth has a fullness to it. If we want to hold it in its essence
and in its entirety, we need to acknowledge all aspects of it, even the
ones we do not like. This is no easy task, but if our intention is to truly
sit on the throne of our lives, then facing ourselves is essential.

For many of us, it's much easier to live in partial truths. It's easier
to blame others than to see ourselves and our shadows. It's more

expedient to medicate ourselves and numb our feelings than to confront what is not working in our lives. It's more fun to surround ourselves with people who agree with us or look like us and indulge our outrage at others' attitudes and behaviors than to try to see the other side—or sides—of things. These partial truths distract us from facing our own complexities and complicities. We put people into simple categories of right and wrong, where it's easy to judge their positions and to overlook what we are contributing to the problem. We say, "We have good values, but you have bad values," or, "My actions are ethical; yours are self-serving," and so on. Have you done that? I have.

It takes our full strength to claim and hold the sword of truth. It means facing our shadows. If we don't, life has a habit of forcing us to reckon with them anyway, putting us into challenging or even painful situations until we realize that we are not blameless. Truth will always confront us, if not now, then at the end of our lives, when we beg for more time to resolve what we haven't yet addressed. When we are brave enough to fully face ourselves in our consistencies and inconsistencies, our courage shows us a new path forward, a new way of connecting and relating to ourselves and others. In divisive times, this full ownership of our lives is crucial.

I have always felt confident expressing my outrage at values I do not agree with, whether they are sexism, racism, or fundamentalism. Yet there came a point when I lost someone dear to me because of my righteous judgment. The painful loss of friendship and love made me wonder if there was a better way for us all to engage our differences.

David had been like a little brother to me. Ten years my junior, David was in his teens when I met him, and I was in my early twenties. It was the early nineties, and I had just moved to Washington, DC. David was interested in international affairs and world politics, and so as I began to travel and work in war zones, I shared stories with him of the people and situations I was encountering. He shared with me his latest political views and what he was studying in school. Since I couldn't see my actual brother who was in Iraq, as travel was banned between the two countries for many years, David took the place of my little brother. My heart would open with joy every time I saw him. I was excited to hear his views as he continued his education, started his career, and explored relationships and romance.

In 2015, when he told me that he had found the woman of his dreams and was getting married, I was over the moon. He seemed very happy, so I was very happy for him, too. Because of my travels, I didn't get to meet Donna before attending the wedding, but afterward I organized an intimate dinner for the three of us to celebrate and to get to know her better.

One of my favorite things to do with people I care about is to share the food I love. I booked a nice table at a Lebanese restaurant. With the small appetizers of hummus, tabbouleh, and fava beans spread beautifully over our table, we started to get to know each other. We talked about how lovely their wedding had been, what they did on their honeymoon, and how they met and fell in love. All was going well. As the waiters brought out the falafel and *fattoush*, our conversation shifted to current events: gay marriage was in the news a lot at that time, and the effects of global warming on the habitats of some endangered species, as well as the role of religion in people's lives.

As we talked, Donna announced that she was absolutely against gay marriage. In fact, she believed homosexual people were doomed to hell. "It's sinful," she declared.

"Why lie about one's sexuality?" I said, responding without thinking much about it. "Isn't it better for a person to be honest about his or her sexual preference rather than suppressing it?"

"Homosexuality is a sin," she responded. "God forbids it."

I was shocked by such a rigid perspective. "To me, it is more important to be truthful to ourselves, to the people around us, and to God rather than denying one's truth and living a lie," I said, my voice becoming less friendly. "The sin is in living a fake life and hurting others in the process, not in being homosexual."

My argument did not work with Donna. She did not want to hear another point of view. The air between us grew cooler. So we switched subjects and moved on to talking about the environment and the animals that were endangered because of global warming. "I love animals so much. I think they are the most honest of all of us," I said.

"You can't equate animals and humans," Donna replied. "We are the superior beings. We have the right to use earth and everything on it for our benefit."

"I disagree," I said, my heart beating faster. "I believe that animals are intelligent, even if we don't know how to understand or value their intelligence." I mentioned how the intelligence of whales, elephants, and crows, for example, has been long studied.

Donna dismissed this. "We don't know for sure. Those studies are just hypotheses."

Donna's views were starting to appall me. Who had David married?

The waiter arrived to clear our appetizers and replace them with entrées. But we ignored the plates of kebab and grilled vegetables as the conversation moved on to the touchy subject of religion. I mentioned the news story about some Catholic priests' molestation of boys. Donna replied sharply, "In our household, we do not criticize religion. We respect it." I struggled to hide my feelings. I hated her views.

We went back and forth—her value, my value; my value, her value—volleying beliefs like we were trading serves in a tennis match. I tried to hold back for the sake of David, but my disdain was clear. My voice rose, and my eyes narrowed. If my words did not communicate my frustration, every part of my demeanor did.

As our conversation grew more and more uncomfortable, David stepped in.

"Don't worry, Zainab," he said, putting his arm around his new wife. "Donna and I agree on these issues. It's okay."

My shock deepened. Maybe David had been trying to cut through the growing tension, but in truth his words disturbed me even more. My beloved friend had these values, too? I questioned whom I had known and loved all these years. After all, he knew my views very well. Even beyond my being an outspoken women's rights advocate, he knew of my commitment to the environment and my love for animals. Had I missed something all along? Who *was* he after all these years? We had always talked openly about politics, religion, and everything else. Nothing had ever been off-limits.

At the end of the evening, we kissed good-night coldly. I was devastated. I had fought with one of my oldest friends. I wondered how his new wife could lack so much compassion. Back at home, I felt so upset that I could not sleep.

Things went from bad to worse. A few weeks later, David wrote me a letter forbidding me from expressing my views to his wife ever again. I was never to talk about any political, religious, social, or environmental issues in their presence. I would be welcomed only if I could chitchat about noncontroversial issues. I knew what this meant. I am not good at small talk, and my entire life is my politics and my views. The political and the personal are intertwined for me. I could never filter what I talked about, even for my closest friend. The choice of either keeping his love and friendship by censoring myself or losing him forever was a tough one—but I couldn't agree to be silent. It would mean betraying myself and everything I stood for.

I chose to lose the friendship and keep my voice, but this choice broke my heart. I lost one of my dearest friends, and that was a high price to pay.

In thinking over this terrible situation, I asked myself if I could have done better in engaging Donna. There was no doubt that the discussion itself was polarizing and I had been strong in my positions. It was also clear that I had not convinced Donna *at all* that my values were the better ones. She hadn't come over to my way of thinking. Instead, I had stood on the "us" side of the argument—the side I thought of as liberal, open-minded, and "good"—and put her on the "them" side, the side of the conservative, close-minded, and "bad." It really hadn't worked.

How can we hold on to our values and still engage people whose values seem to oppose ours? Could I have not just crusaded with my political values but also tried harder to relate to Donna on things that she might have valued, too? And what *was* the full truth that I was not seeing? I knew why I found people like her and their perspectives irritating and arrogant, but what were they seeing in me that was irritating to them? What was I missing?

I told a trusted friend, a psychologist, about the unpleasant meal I'd shared with Donna, about how I'd disagreed with her and how I'd lost David's love. My friend nodded in an understanding way. "Are you willing to go into your own shadow as a way to understanding her shadow?" he asked. He explained how going into our own darkness, seeing it, understanding it, can help us see and understand the darkness in others. The journey starts with knowing that we, too, have darkness inside us and exploring what it is in our own lives.

My friend's explanation reminded me of a South Indian story in Coleman Barks's translation of Rumi poems, *The Essential Rumi*. The story goes that "soap is the dirt we buy." As we introduce soap to the dirt we are trying to clean, the two dirts mix and neutralize each other. My shadow was my dirt. If I want to clean the world of "dirt," perhaps I needed to start by understanding my own dirt.

The inward journey is not an easy one. To see our dark truths, we need to explore our own shadow, stay open to what we see, and resist judging it. If I wanted to truly see without judgment, I would need an attitude of curiosity. I knew from my work in different cultures that whenever I came in with judgment, it drew thick curtains across any true understanding. Only when I relaxed and allowed curiosity to lead could I understand certain traditions or practices from a fresh perspective. Could I apply this knowledge to myself now? Could I see my shadow without judgment, not to justify it, but to understand it?

I decided to do a simple ritual taught to me years ago by Angeles Arrien, a teacher of indigenous traditions. I cleaned my house and bathed myself, repeating my intention to explore my darkness and to stay curious no matter what came up. In the peace and privacy of my home, I made a comfortable place to lie down. I lit candles and selected some powerful music to immerse myself in—my favorite, Ennio Morricone's soundtrack to *The Mission*. This way, with the help of the music, I could slow down enough to explore the places I had not wanted to go to inside myself.

I lay down, closed my eyes, and listened as the music began to surge. I took a deep breath and let my imagination fly. As the images came, I let them wash over me. A hawk was flying over a field, its wings ruffling in the wind; a horse was running through the field; the field was morphing into a cave—the images were appearing, changing, and dissolving like images in a dream. I followed them from one to the other, fully relaxed and in full trust. Eventually, I saw a place I had no idea existed within me: a place of arrogance. *Me? Arrogant? Impossible!*

I contracted from this insight. I rejected it. But I remembered my commitment not to judge. I went back into the process. *So what was this arrogance?*

My arrogance was like a teenage bully who took whatever it wanted without regard for anyone else. It was entitled, confident, and loud. I allowed myself to be in it fully—and I loved it. I loved not caring about how others might feel. I loved taking whatever I wanted with no guilt or self-doubt. In surrendering to the arrogance, I could see how others felt they could grab whatever they wanted—a piece of land, a tank, a machine gun—without any hesitation, remorse, or worry. I heard myself yell, "Give me that. It is mine now!" It felt great. Arrogance brought all the ugly aspects of me out and celebrated them. It did not care about people's judgments whatsoever, for it knew their ugly sides and brought them out, too. My arrogance was bold, strong, and audacious. I did not want to stop. I felt completely powerful and completely free.

In that deep place within, I wondered, *If this feels so great, what is the incentive to change? Who would give up this kind of arrogance if there were no repercussions?*

Going even deeper, I asked, *What is this arrogance trying to cover up?* I saw anger at all the injustice in the world. If bringing justice to injustice was the light I brought to the world, my arrogance and shadow told me that things are always unjust, and the only way people could thrive was to be part of the injustice. *No one cares!* it said. In that space, I could understand the militiaman holding his gun and killing people in Iraq or DR Congo or South Sudan. I could understand how they derived a sense of power from their violence, not only with their guns but also by seeing through the corruption of power in others. They named what was ugly in others and embraced it. It was the way to be and get ahead in an unfair world.

In that moment, I saw that behind all that arrogance in myself was a deep insecurity, fear, and pain. The arrogance felt like a mask that I was wearing to hide a deformed part of me, a mask of strength to protect an inner ugliness from exposure. I was afraid that as an ambitious woman I was unlovable; I was afraid that as a single woman I would not have material security; I felt insecure about not being beautiful; I was full of rage at the destruction of my country, Iraq, from the Gulf Wars; I was disgusted by those who were oblivious to that destruction and the pain it has caused millions of people. I had pushed all these fears, insecurities, and angers down deep inside me. There they festered.

That's when the light bulb went on. I was too embarrassed to talk about all my fear, insecurity, and anger, but these feelings were alive in my shadow. I saw that things do not die in darkness. I may have buried my issues, but they were very much alive and wanted to be acknowledged. These ugly parts of me *wanted* to be seen, not stifled. My arrogance was like the lid on my lockbox. It held down the intensity of these raw, "unacceptable" feelings.

It was love that held me throughout this inward journey. I had to trust in my basic goodness. Otherwise, I would have gotten lost in the darkness and confusion of what I was seeing; I would have abandoned my explorations when they got uncomfortable. Looking inward at our deepest truths can be disorienting. When all felt dark, anchoring myself in love was my saving grace. It allowed me to come through all the fear that arose.

Remembering that I was basically a good person gave me access to more insights, too. I realized that the only way I could stop the damage being done by my powerful, hungry shadow was by respecting it rather than hiding it. If I gave it some room, acknowledged it, and had a genuine conversation with it, then I could bring it out of the box where I'd locked it up for so long. By owning it, I would also prevent others from manipulating it for their own interests. I would have nothing to hide anymore. I would have to hold my shadow next to my light as I engaged with the world rather than lead only with my light. I would have to admit, "Yes, I am insecure about my looks, but that's for me to process, not for the advertising industry to manipulate. Yes, I'm furious about what men do to women, but that does not mean that I will punish men as if they all lack humanity. Yes, I'm devastated by the state of destruction in Iraq, but I refuse to indulge in hate for the sake of revenge."

Whatever is ugly in us does not dare express itself freely. It knows it is unacceptable. But it craves the light. Understanding this, I could finally understand those people I considered misguided, like Donna, or unfathomable, like religious fundamentalists: they were acting out of their shadows. Some knew they were, and some didn't. Those who didn't know remained terrified of their shadows and unwilling to admit they had them. Others relished their shadows, used them, and manipulated the darkness of others to get what they wanted—usually power and attention. The few who knew both their shadows and their light, I saw, were fully claiming their swords of truth.

✱

As I struggled with my loss of David's friendship and processed the meaning of my hidden arrogance, I thought of Rami Elhanan. Rami was an Israeli father whose fourteen-year-old daughter had been killed by two Palestinian suicide bombers. She had been riding a city bus with a couple of friends to buy books for school when the bus exploded. Rami had grown up in Jerusalem, as a loyal citizen in a Zionist household. He had served in the Israeli army and was proud of his country. He saw himself as defending Israel and his family from Palestinians, who, he was taught, had an inferior culture and base values.

When his daughter was killed, his heart was torn open. In the midst of his pain, he asked himself a question that had never occurred to him before: *Why do the Palestinians hate us so much?* His daughter was just an innocent teenage girl, after all. She wasn't a soldier or a vigilante. She had no agenda. *Why would Palestinians hate her so much they'd kill themselves to take her life? Why were they fighting with everything they had—with stones, bombs, and human lives? Why were they so angry?* To answer these questions, he went into his rage and pain, to where his own inner "enemy" lived, to find out how to relate to the feelings and the drive of these people whose actions had hurt him so deeply. It meant questioning what he'd been taught his entire life.

Rami started reaching out to Palestinian parents who had also lost their children. He joined the Parents Circle, a group of six-hundred-plus bereaved Israeli and Palestinian families who had all lost family in the seemingly endless conflict between their nations. By crossing checkpoints into Palestinian territories in the West Bank to talk to parents, he began to understand their losses and their anger. He heard stories of a nine-year-old Palestinian girl shot in the head by an Israeli soldier as she came out of school during a curfew; a sixteen-year-old Palestinian boy imprisoned for two years for demonstrating with a Palestinian flag in the street with a handful of his high school friends during a curfew; a Palestinian mother who lost her baby when she was not allowed across a checkpoint during childbirth.

After hearing many, many stories of Palestinian grievances, Rami started seeing what he had never known of the reality that Palestinians live in. His eyes were opened to who the "enemy"—whom he'd hated before—actually was. They were ordinary people like him whose homes were demolished while extended families still lived inside them; they were whole villages and towns cut off by giant walls so that people could not leave to work or support themselves.

Instead of hating the faceless Palestinian aggressors and wanting to kill them for killing his daughter, Rami started to stand alongside them. Working together with them in this way gave him a reason to get up in the morning. As he journeyed toward truth, Rami realized that as a proud Israeli, he had actually protected his ignorance of Palestinians. He had his reasons for loving his country, but over the years that love and the need to protect it had become rigid. His position and his identity had become dogmatic. He wondered why he hadn't asked himself these questions about Palestinians before.

When we don't see our own shadows, we act out of those shadows and inevitably inflict pain on others, even if that's not our intention. We can even become oppressors or aggressors ourselves. When we tell ourselves our story over and over again, justifying it and demonizing anyone who does not share it, we can harden into an identity that does not allow for the complexities of real-life situations. It's the easiest thing to polarize our perspectives, to take a position and then never budge from it.

But when we *do* see our shadows, real change and real connection become possible. Allowing ourselves to ask questions begins to breach the walls of opposition and hatred. We lift up the lids of our locked boxes and dare to look inside. This is how we overcome the fear, hatred, and even cruelty that may be hidden within us.

Seeing how arrogance lived deep inside myself, I became even more curious about how I could take full responsibility for this shadow in me. How could I genuinely connect with those whose values I couldn't agree with? I kept asking, How could I have compassion for the people around me whom I saw as "other"? How could I see things from their perspectives?

The idea of finding common ground didn't appeal to me. There is no common ground between those who think homosexuality is a sin and those who do not; or between those who believe that it is okay to kill for power and those who do not; or between men who believe it is their right to grab women however they want and those who believe that no such right exists. But I was curious to know how the other side sees the world in ways that I did not. That understanding, I saw, was the first step in learning how to engage differently.

As a women's rights activist, I was fueled for a long time by my anger at men and the injustice they created for women. I had plenty of reasons to be angry—at the violence women endure in war and in peace, at the mass rapes, at the discrimination, at the marginalization of women's voices, at the social codes that demand female silence. Abuse of women and girls happens around the world, in Europe, Africa, the Middle East, Asia, North and South America—everywhere—and the majority of this abuse, violence, and neglect comes from men. I chose to work in the parts of the world where that violence was most obvious—in war zones, where violence against women is not nuanced. It is as clear as sunlight. My anger at men was as clear as sunlight, too.

That anger sometimes snuck into the way I treated the men around me, even those I loved very much, such as my friends, brothers, and father. I would feel it bubble up whenever they made a simplistic comment on women's issues or laughed at a sexist joke; whenever they didn't like a movie with a female character who was oppressed, or sympathized with a man who snapped at his wife, or felt that a woman had wronged them. Even at these times, I felt like a crusader against men for their oppression of women. I could not reconcile my anger with my love for the men closest to me.

I carried this conflict in me for many years, unable to acknowledge it even to myself. My rage *was* easily justified, and it motivated me to work very hard. But over time it also started to alienate me from the other side of the issue—from men's real stories. I had gotten to a place where I just wanted to punish men; I was not at all interested in their humanity.

Then, I had an encounter that, like a mirror of truth, led me to a startling realization. In my anger at men, I was risking becoming the very thing I despised: the oppressor. I was fighting so hard against stereotyping women as just victims without voices to speak back to the powers that abused them, I saw all men as only aggressors who always abused. I had never stopped to consider the possibility that a man could also be suffering, that he might want to atone for his transgressions, and, more than that, that he could already be an ally.

This realization came while I was working at a displaced people's camp in Afghanistan, not long after the United States and the international community arrived, shortly after September 11, 2001. Like many camps, it was a vast scene of tents, with children playing in the makeshift roads and laundry drying on ropes that wove through the site. It was miles and miles of lightly organized chaos in the midst of the desert, from tent to tent, person to person, story to story.

I was standing with an Afghan colleague from Women for Women International as we finished a few hours of interviewing women to see what further services we could provide to help them. That's when I saw two Afghan men in the distance walking slowly toward us. I could just make out their long beards and turbans. In my mind, that meant the Taliban. I wanted to leave as soon as I spotted them. I felt they were walking toward us to hurt us, kill us, or kidnap us. I was clearly a foreign woman in the sea of Afghans. My attempts to blend in could never fully disguise me.

"Let's get in the car and get out of here as fast as we can," I whispered to Sweeta. "These men are here to kill us."

"We can't," she answered, holding my hand tightly. "We must stay. If we leave, we will make people suspicious of us and never be able to enter the camp to help these women again. We must meet these men and understand what they want from us."

I could see her point, and despite my fear, I stood still. I trusted her judgment, but it felt like a huge risk. We were putting our lives on the line without knowing if we were making the right decision. My throat was dry, and my hands were shaking. The men were walking and walking toward us, coming into sharper focus as they left the vast, silent desert behind, like a mirage slowly transforming into reality. The quiet was intoxicating, dizzying. With each step they took toward us, my heart beat faster.

Then, they arrived. I fought my urge to run.

"We want to thank you for helping our wives," the older one said slowly and deliberately as both men put out their hands to shake ours. "This program is making them happy and is feeding our families, and for that we are grateful."

The man's words hit me like a punch in the stomach. I took their hands in mine, trembling with relief. I smiled and talked with them, but I was also trying to hide my shock. It was their traditional Afghan look that made me think they were Taliban—the same hats, pants, tunics, and beards. Not only were they not Taliban, they were victims of the Taliban themselves! These men and their families had been terrorized and displaced by the fundamentalists for years. The men's clothes were just a reflection of that region in Afghanistan, not of their political stance.

It was in that moment that I caught my own prejudice. I had stereotyped these Afghans. It was deeply ironic: my whole life was about fighting stereotypes. I fought for the world to see women survivors of war as full humans, not just victims. I wanted the world to see beyond that frozen image of women's suffering and to listen to women's voices and opinions instead and let them contribute to building peace. I knew the danger of stereotypes. But in that moment, I had actually assumed these men were aggressors, murderers, rapists, based on their looks and my fears.

Instead, these men were kind, warm, and caring. They spoke of their concerns for the women and told us about the hardships they had been through. When they said how grateful they felt as husbands to see our organization helping their wives be happy, I felt a weight in my chest: what courage it took for these men to thank a group of women for providing something that they could not. The men had been stripped of the means to provide for their families. They had been emasculated by other men more powerful than they. I had not even had the courage to wait to hear what they had to say.

That experience made me realize I needed to reach out to men in the war zones I was working in and try to hear them, try to understand what went on inside their heads and their hearts, even when they were violent. If I wanted to stop violence against women, then I needed to talk to men and engage them in that process. To do that, I needed to change my attitude from anger to compassion. That transformation had to happen in my heart, not only in my words. Otherwise I would continue to overlook the good men, the kind men, and men's anguish and complexities.

My newfound desire to understand men's perspectives didn't weaken my commitment to women's rights and freedom, and it certainly didn't mean forgetting the past and allowing men's violence against women to continue. But it did compel me to look at my work in a different way. I was less locked, rigid, shrill, and fixed in my ideas. I found I was able to open my heart and listen to the stories of anyone who was willing to talk to me, including the worst of them—the rapists, pimps, and killers.

When I started speaking to men and listening carefully to what they were going through, I saw that, just like the women I worked with, they were not permitted to stray from the script society had given them. Women survivors of war were often not fully seen by society or by the humanitarian community that was there to help them. They ceased to have their own identities or the ability to forge their own futures. Their primary role was to suffer, cry, and silently clean up the destruction. The men, for their part, were allowed nothing but to be strong and tough. No one talked to them about their pain and loss. They were expected simply to swallow it. They were supposed to work, find food, and kill, but they were left in an emotional black hole.

It was a Bosnian man from Sarajevo who further opened my eyes to the diversity of men's experiences and feelings. It started with my simple need to get a massage when I was working in the aftermath of war-torn Sarajevo. My colleague recommended someone—Nusrat, a very tall, very full man. If his physique was big, even intimidating, his facial features were soft and welcoming. He had warm eyes, a very kind smile, and salt-and-pepper hair that fell to his shoulders.

The massage happened in silence in his studio. After, he offered to drive me to my hotel, as he was already going in that direction. We got into his old red Reno, a car that had obviously survived a lot during the war. It was a small car and only just fit a man as big as Nusrat. There was not even an inch left for him to move. During the ride, I asked him about his life, what he did before the war, and if he was in Sarajevo during the war.

"I was, and it was a very hard time for me," Nusrat answered.

I immediately assumed he was talking about the siege of Sarajevo, the terrible cold and hunger that people suffered, so I commented on that. But he corrected me.

"Yes, these were all very tough, but what was tougher is that I couldn't fight. We were surrounded by snipers who were shooting us like animals in cages. Bosnian men and women tried to do everything to defend ourselves. We made weapons from kitchen supplies, we dug underground tunnels with forks and shovels, and many men volunteered to fight with whatever weapons we had. But I couldn't. I was given a machine gun, trained how to use it, sat behind it with my finger on the trigger, but I couldn't shoot. I just couldn't kill any human being, even if it was in self-defense."

"That is totally understandable. I know I couldn't kill either," I responded.

"Not when you are a man. Other men laughed at me. They ridiculed me for my inability to kill, for my emotions, for my rejection of the machine gun. They assigned me to cooking, which I did willingly, but I could never look at them in the eyes. I was their laughingstock."

Nusrat did not care that he couldn't kill; he was shamed and humiliated by his countrymen. His pain was in being ridiculed. As we arrived my hotel, I thanked Nusrat not only for the wonderful massage but also for the story he shared. Hearing his story and understanding his pain were helping to heal my heart. I would never have known that men carried this kind of anguish. I was seeing firsthand that not all men were the same—they had different emotions and intentions and drives, yet I had been grouping them together as one.

Not long after, I heard a story that helped push me to find understanding—though not forgiveness—for even the most degraded man. I was in Baghdad, working at the Women for Women International offices. We heard of a sixteen-year-old girl who had been kidnapped and raped when security forces collapsed soon after the US invasion and militias emerged to rule the streets. Rape was a routine matter for militia fighters, in Iraq and in every war zone—it was how they dominated and demoralized people and expressed their power.

Accompanied by colleagues, I went to this young woman's home to interview her to see how we could help. She cried as she described how men came in the middle of the night and dragged her and her sister from their bed, where they were asleep with their mother. In their hideout, the kidnappers discussed what price they could get if they sold the two girls as virgins or if they raped them first.

"The big guy, who seemed to be the boss of the group, decided he wanted to rape me. So he dragged me to the other room, forced me to lie down on a sofa, and got on top of me. He started to unzip his trousers. I was crying and begging, 'Please, please don't rape me. Don't you have a heart?' He looked straight into my eyes and said, 'My heart died a long time ago.' And then he raped me," she whispered.

I cried for this girl and for the terror and pain that she had suffered. But this time I cried for the aggressor, too. I suddenly realized that even a monstrous rapist could be in an even more perilous situation than his victim. He was locked into darkness, unable to change. The girl was hurt, no question, but her soul was intact, and with help, I knew, she could rebuild her inner strength. The man who raped her, though, had lost his soul, and such a loss has no repair. For this, I had compassion. I felt anguish for what he could never get back: his very humanity. When even one of us is consumed by such ugly cruelty it is indeed a big loss for all of us.

It can be very hard to hear the other side, but I knew that if we wanted true transformation, we could not ignore men's stories. I continued to meet men who would talk to me, fighters and executioners who were open to my questions. As they would tell me the horrific things they had done, my heart would race. But I still wanted to understand what they were they trying to get, what drove them, what made them afraid, and what they held in their hearts. If I was to promote true healing, I had to help create a new culture, one where a man could define his own identity and where the son did not blindly repeat his father's crimes. I had to show empathy and acceptance to the son and his father. Not out of blindness and forgetting, but out of understanding the patterns that lead individuals to behave the way they do.

It was a hard path to walk between believing—truly believing—that a criminal must be punished for his crime and yet still developing compassion for him so he might find a path to return to society. It was not easy to bring these values together in my heart. Yet I was no longer able to continue fighting for women's rights from the same place of anger. When anger drove me, I became the very tyrant I was trying to fight against. Anger is important for igniting the fire to fight injustice, but it can never be the fuel that sustains the burning. By itself, anger can lead to reactionary behavior, entrenchment, and more crimes; it can end up burning everything, even that which we are fighting *for*. My anger alone was not enough to fight injustice.

As a result, I decided that it was time to start showing men, in a language they understood, why women's voices and rights were so important, not only to women but to them as well. We worked in collaboration with religious and militia leaders from countries that had high rates of violence against women, like DR Congo and Afghanistan, and started to talk about the issues from men's perspectives. I remember meeting with a group in Rwanda. About fifteen men gathered and sat together on the ground, chitchatting about farming, the weather, and other things.

I asked them, "Tell me, why do some men beat their wives?"

At first the men laughed and shifted uncomfortably.

"I am asking because I really want to understand men's perspectives," I said. The men laughed again.

As the laughter faded into silence, one young man spoke up: "There are days in which I can't find work. These days I come home empty-handed. I have no money to buy food for the family. When I hear my wife say, 'The children are hungry,' she shames me for not being a good father. Then I start beating her."

It is too simple to say what is behind domestic violence is shame like this man's. But maybe behind domestic violence is *pain*, and if our goal is to stop the violence, then we need to ask how we can engage this kind of pain differently. Maybe, I thought, I have been so driven by the moral reasons to stop violence against women, especially during war, that I've overlooked what drives men. Maybe they were not driven by moral reasons. In war, living in extreme poverty and vulnerability can change people's morality. What if I showed men practical and pragmatic reasons to change their behavior, instead? If my goal was to find ways to immediately stop the abuse of the women I was working with, then maybe I needed a different approach.

I worked with my team to develop a training program for men that would show how they could be better leaders, have more success, and lead healthier lives when they stopped their violence. It demonstrated the potential losses and gains of their behavior in terms that made sense to them. A year after one of these trainings, a rebel leader in DR Congo sat in front of me with his military boots on, machine gun on the side, and said, "Before I took this program, every time I entered the house of a man who did not have a gun when I did have a gun, I raped his wife. I never thought twice about it. In this program I learned I could get HIV, infect all my family, and kill them. I could lose my soldiers to HIV, too. So I stopped raping because I don't want to die nor lose my men. That led me to spend more time with my wife. Over time our relationship, which was distant before, improved. We started trusting each other and eventually saving our money together. We bought a better house, and life got better. Now, I spend my spare time talking to soldiers and telling them they can improve their lives if they stop raping and spend more time with their wives."

My heart bounded with fear as I listened to this guy's story. I feared his military boots, fatigues, and guns; his presence felt very intimidating and unsafe. But he was indeed helping to stop the immediate violence against women. I still believed he should be brought to trial to be prosecuted and punished for his past violence. But until then, his change of behavior and attitude was having an immediate positive effect: it was stopping violence against women. That was my priority for the women I was serving.

The changes I'd hoped for happened. First, they came out of men's self-interest. But later, when the men had more time with their families, better lives, more money, peace, and success, the changes happened within their own leadership. I wondered, what if behind *all* our fears was the simple desire to be accepted? What if there was a route to that acceptance through love, not fear?

＊

On reflection, I could see that I had led more with fear than with love during my dinner with Donna and David. Since that friendship had soured, I wasn't likely to get another chance to speak to them or reattempt our conversation, as much as my heart might long for it. But I had plenty of chances to speak to people of different values in the rest of my life. A little while after that inward journey in my living room, I was invited to a small private dinner in an affluent area of Connecticut. At the dinner, I was seated across from a very conservative woman whose son was working locally as a chief of staff to one of the guests. She'd come to visit from Washington State. She was neatly dressed, but her hair and her clothes showed that she was from a humble background, not like the people at this upscale dinner.

The conversation turned to the recent discussion of Muslims in America and whether they were a threat to US security, as some politicians were arguing. The issue was dominating the news at that moment. Most of the people at the dinner, being left leaning, were making jokes about how ludicrous it was. I noticed that Sally wasn't saying anything. So I started to engage her. I had just been interviewing people in Minnesota about their worries that more Muslim immigrants would bring repressive ways to America.

At first, as a Muslim myself, I found these views extremely offensive. They were built on hurtful stereotypes; it's impossible to generalize about an entire group of people. But I knew I had to listen and engage with understanding and compassion if I wanted my own point of view to be heard. I told Sally about the interviews and what fears people had shared. "Do you share some of these fears, Sally?"

She nodded in agreement. I paused and took a deep breath.

"I know, the news is always giving us reasons to fear Muslims," I said. "Tell me about what makes *you* afraid?" I had no idea if Sally knew that I was a Muslim American, originally from Iraq. In that crowd, she might have just assumed that I was as much a misfit as she was.

She told me she was afraid that Muslims would bring Shari'a to America, that they would oppress their wives, sisters, and daughters, and that they might impose the same oppression on American women. Instead of charging forward in frustration and anger in that moment, I figured out which of her fears I could connect to and spoke to that.

"You're afraid that if more Muslims come here," I said in a neutral tone, "that they will change your community."

Yes, she said. Her town was small, rural, mostly white, and mostly Republican. She didn't want American values of freedom and democracy to be threatened by fanaticism. It was hard to stomach, as I knew that many Muslims had come to America fleeing the oppression of dictatorship, authoritarian regimes, war, and fundamentalists and cherished the opportunity they'd been given to live in safety and peace. Many more still were American born and raised and identified fully as United States citizens. Still, I did understand Sally's concerns. After all, some violent attacks have happened in the name of Islam. I myself had been afraid of attacks by Islamic radicals.

My understanding had an immediate effect: when she knew I wasn't going to shut her down, Sally relaxed. When she felt that I heard and understood her, she lowered her defenses and her fixed attachment to her opinions. She could hear me in ways she likely would not have if I had just reacted and lashed out. Acknowledging that "I hear you," I realized, is not the same as agreeing.

"I am Muslim, you know," I said. "I can tell you that Shari'a is not a constitution; it's not even a book. It's an interpretation of the religion that changes from one country to the next and from one time in history to another. It's true that some fundamentalists use it for their own interests, but it really plays no role in the vast majority of Muslims' lives. Certainly not in my life nor in the lives of millions of Muslims in America."

Sally was listening. I told her that women wearing head scarves are not necessarily doing it because their families are forcing them.

Some *American-born* Muslim women are wearing it as a way of protesting the stereotypes of them. They're making the point that they should be accepted as Muslims *and* as Americans. Others, like me, do not wear the head scarf and don't believe in it. "I am a Muslim woman, and I am not oppressed." I said with a smile.

Now, Sally started to ask questions about Muslims that she had always wondered about. What was their belief in God? Was Islam a violent religion or peaceful one? What does Islam stand for? In another time of my life I would have answered with antagonism and frustration. We started talking and laughing as she asked questions and I tried to answer them, each exchange building grace and love between us.

"You know, Sally, American Muslims are also afraid of other Americans who are attacking them and saying they should all go back. For immigrants like me, this country is a refuge. When other people realize we are Muslim, we fear we will be attacked."

"You're absolutely right," Sally said. "We are all just feeding into each other's fears!"

Our conversation, which could have exploded into a heated argument with lots of finger-pointing, just like my conversation with Donna had, became a dialogue. We became two people sharing their fears—sharing the complexities of emotions rather than taking a hard stand from our fixed positions.

As our talk came to a close, she said, "I really appreciate that you did not accuse me of racism and prejudice. You allowed me to address my issues myself. Thank you."

I was moved by our conversation and appreciated Sally's openness and graciousness. We had built a bridge.

Holding our sword of truth means not *only* speaking from our true values but speaking from our true vulnerabilities as well. The connections between us are these very vulnerabilities, beyond our political, religious, or cultural positions. Sally and I were politically opposite, but we found a way to connect. The men I encountered in war zones were not all monsters—and I was not all good, myself. From this awareness, I could clearly see that if we continued only to point our fingers at one another, we were in danger of losing sight of ourselves as humans, good humans who essentially believe in doing good and in showing love and kindness in our daily lives, no matter where we are on the political spectrum.

What if another way of engaging is in being extremely authentic about our feelings, as well as being loyal to our values? Can we transform our fixed positions into flexible identities? Can we be like Rami, the Israeli father, and acknowledge how our ingrained perspectives might unknowingly hurt others? Can we not be driven by our fear and insecurity so that we become violent and oppressive ourselves? Do we have to wait for terrible loss to truly see how our own attitudes and actions contribute to the destruction of what we love?

Let's tell the full truth on a human scale, on a personal scale, instead of barking our positions from our self-righteous identities. If someone is against abortion in his politics, will he refuse to support his sister when it becomes dangerous for her to bring a pregnancy to full term? What if her pregnancy was the result of rape? Would he keep his hard line against abortion then? When we see the complexities of real-life circumstances, will we choose to have compassion, or will we rigidly hold to our party line?

What if the woman accusing her boss of harassment also reflects on how she flirted with him as a way to move up in the company? Yes, men traditionally have abused their power. Yes, men have objectified and sexualized women instead of seeing them as full human beings. But as women, have we resorted to the age-old arts of seduction to get what we wanted when we were not treated equally? We need to ask: Where have we sold ourselves out? That's our shadow.

If we don't see that shadow and take responsibility for how it plays out in our actions and decisions, we're in danger of abusing our individual power. At the same time, we undermine the legitimacy of our grievances.

This is how we can claim our sword of truth—not in moral outcry, but by showing up in our vulnerabilities and fears, and in our inconsistencies as well. The fuller truth is that we are angry both at the perpetrator for abusing us and at ourselves for allowing the abuse. The fuller truth is that life is complex, and *positions* are not emotions. We all feel pain when we lose love. We all fear change.

The unknown makes us nervous. No one wants to be molested, abused, or harassed. We feel embarrassed when we allow ourselves to be bought or silenced. We enjoy power. We are afraid to die. The sword of truth is about showing up with the integrity of the full truth itself, the good, the bad, *and* the ugly—inside of us, not just out there in the world.

When we speak up and stand up, acknowledge our shadows, we will face all the feelings that we've locked up inside: all the embarrassment, desire, instability, anger, or whatever has been hidden for so long. As uncomfortable as it is for a time, we also free ourselves—because then we really own ourselves. Others cannot control or blackmail us. We grow in the process, becoming an example of what is possible when we take ownership of ourselves and our lives.

Only when we see the full picture more clearly can we learn a new way to fight the larger darkness in our world. We can have compassion not only for people we know and understand but for those whom we disagree with as well. If we want to stop the bully, we need to understand how the bully lives in ourselves, too. Then we can have a new dialogue that stems, not out of an "I am good and you are bad" dichotomy, but out of an acknowledgment of whom we are fully.

I have come to understand that the bullies in the world are themselves the masks for what is ugly in our societies. They take on our darkness because we refuse to do it. When *only* the bully is willing to acknowledge what's ugly, then he or she is the one who controls our shadows. He or she can manipulate us, because we ourselves refuse to face our dark truths. We lose control of them, helplessly, angrily pointing our fingers at *him*, projecting our loss of control onto *her*.

The only way to take this manipulating out of the hands of the bullies is for all of us to create a space to talk about what is ugly in us as individuals and in us as a collective.

We can meet the darkness of others only when we go into our own darkness first. I hope that one day I will be reunited with David and Donna and will have the chance to meet them in love and in my fullness.

6

Forgiving Ourselves First

Only when we clean out our old clutter
can new dreams arrive.

W e must forgive even when we are not asked for forgiveness." This sentence popped into my mind as I reached a state of deep silence during a meditation retreat. At first, I tried to brush the thought away. *That is too much to ask.* Giving forgiveness to those who apologize is one thing, but when forgiveness is not even asked for? That is quite another thing. To ask those who have been cheated, betrayed, or lost trust to forgive in their hearts without any acknowledgment or remorse from the other side? *No—too much to ask.* Yet the thought rose again from that silent space. "We must forgive even when not asked for forgiveness." It kept insisting that I recognize it.

After the meditation, I continued to struggle with the concept. Forgiveness is a noble idea, but easier to talk about than to practice authentically. We admire it and advocate for it intellectually. We buy fridge magnets with slogans of forgiveness on them, we post about forgiveness on our Facebook pages, and we study those who embody forgiveness, such as Nelson Mandela or the Dalai Lama. But when it comes to forgiving the real people in our lives—the partners who have cheated on us, friends who have deceived us, or colleagues who have betrayed us—we realize how much harder it is to put into practice. Sometimes we say the words "I forgive you," but our hearts stay cold. Sometimes we try to put a hurt behind us, thinking that is enough, but we don't truly process it or forgive the one who hurt us. Sometimes the pain lingers in our hearts for so long that it becomes part of the intimate story of who we are.

Much of our world's history rests on hurt and betrayal that have not been truly forgiven. Resentments are carried through generations. Families, cities, countries, and peoples all carry unforgiven divides. We see examples all around us—between African Americans and European Americans, between indigenous peoples and settlers, between Palestinians and Israelis, and so many more. There are even ancient animosities between men and women. One day we are kissing and loving and marrying one another, and the next day we are mortal enemies. At times we can let the past go and not dwell on it. At other times the ancient tensions rise up and spark new unrest on top of the old wounds. These divides can seem entrenched and impossible to resolve. Cynics say that forgiveness is a nice idea, but it can never work to resolve such deep-seated pain.

I have no answers to the cynics. I do know that in historic moments when truth, reconciliation, and forgiveness have been practiced—such as in South Africa and Rwanda—it was initiated by the victims, not the aggressors. In both cases, forgiveness was meant to lift the burden of the past so that everyone, especially the victims, could start on a new path forward. In forgiveness there is a freedom from the pain that we carry from being so deeply hurt. It's a pain that shows itself in our bodies, in our souls, and in our psyches. I knew the concept intellectually but not emotionally for the longest time.

The only way to truly practice forgiveness is to put ourselves on the line in a personal way and find out how it feels in our own hearts. We need to grant forgiveness for the most intimate hurts that we've suffered and ask to be forgiven for the hurts that we've caused. If we can forgive each other in the small ways of our lives, we can find out how to forgive the big stories of our peoples and our histories, too.

It takes the same emotional muscle for us to forgive someone who has betrayed our trust as it does for a nation to forgive another nation or for women to forgive men. It takes the same courage to ask to be forgiven as it does to acknowledge our role in whatever larger stories have divided us for centuries. Forgiving means softening the fixed identities that make us who we are as women or men, Eastern or Western, white or black. It means rewriting our stories to the positive, sweeping clean our hurt and resentment. It means gently erasing the histories that have shaped us, the way rivers shape the ground they pass over. Can we truly forgive and let go of that past—forever? Can our rivers run in new directions?

Forgiveness can be heard only when it is given or offered sincerely. I learned this when I was allowed to observe a *gacaca* court session in Rwanda in the mid-2000s. In 1994, a Hutu extremist organization known as Interahamwe incited genocide against the Tutsi minority in Rwanda. In the killing frenzy that followed, Hutu butchered their fellow citizens, hunting them with machetes, setting fire to farms, homes, and churches—sometimes with people locked inside—destroying everyone and everything they could. Hutu husbands killed their Tutsi wives, priests killed parishioners, neighbors killed neighbors. Bodies were left piled in the streets and churches. Countless children were orphaned, up to half a million women were raped, and nearly one million people were killed in just one hundred days.

The destruction was mind-boggling. The number of accused perpetrators topped one hundred thousand. There were not enough jails to hold them nor enough lawyers and judges left alive to run the trials. If Rwandans had used the modern Western-style court system to process all of the accused, it would have taken decades. Instead, they resorted to the gacaca courts, the almost forgotten tradition of holding court "in the grass." In villages all over the country, respected leaders gathered outside among their communities to listen to perpetrators recount their crimes. Victims and witnesses would tell their versions of what happened as well. If the community elders felt that the perpetrator had admitted and acknowledged his crime sincerely and was ready to be reintegrated back into the community, they would try to find an appropriate sentence. In all cases, perpetrators would have to face and serve their victims every day. The retribution came from showing up, over and over again, to help those they had harmed: to show up for the child or elderly person whose family no longer existed, for the woman whose rape resulted in a child, or for the man who had been crippled in an attack. Sentences were geared toward helping rebuild the community and repairing as much physical and moral damage as possible.

This community-court model allowed Rwandans to start dealing with the crimes sooner. State, national, and international courts were clogged up with more major criminals: the Interahamwe commanders who had ordered the genocide. Appearing in the community courts did not necessarily mean a lesser sentence, since perpetrators had to acknowledge their heinous crimes in front of everyone they knew—families, neighbors, friends, and people they had grown up with. It did mean a different way of going about justice and retribution outside of the prison system.

I was allowed to observe the gacaca court one afternoon in a small village surrounded by Rwanda's famous hills. I had been invited because I was working with women in some nearby communities to help them rebuild their lives financially and emotionally. The villagers looked at me curiously, since generally no foreigners were allowed to attend the courts; these community reckonings were very private events. I joined the women and men in their colorful printed shirts and beautiful tie-dyed wrap skirts and head wraps, doing my best to keep a low profile.

The accused came one by one, wearing the identifying prison garb of pink shirts and shorts. First, a man confessed to burning down his neighbor's farm. The elders listened to him, took a few moments to consult with one another, then came back with his sentence: he was to work for free farming his neighbor's land until the farm was once again a lush coffee and tea plantation. The next man talked about how he had killed a Tutsi woman's son. The court sentenced him to act as a son to the bereaved mother, providing all the financial support and physical help that an able-bodied man would.

Then came a man who described how he had killed his neighbor, destroyed property, and led Interahamwe to the hideout of a group of unarmed women and children, who were then slaughtered. His stories were vivid, but his storytelling lacked any feeling. He narrated every detail like a robot—"I did this, and I did that," as if to say, "Yes, I did these things, but my crimes were not as bad as other people's."

He showed little remorse. The elders listened, asked some questions, and heard from witnesses. Then they announced a break to consult with one another about his sentence.

Rwanda is a beautiful country, with red mud earth, a deeply blue sky, and vegetation of every shade of green across its thousands of hills. Its beauty made for a dizzying contrast to the disturbing crimes people were describing having committed. As we waited for the verdict, I wondered what punishment this man would receive. How would the council handle what seemed like a lack of feeling for the people who had suffered because of him?

When the elders came back from deliberating, their spokeswoman addressed the man: "We do not feel sincerity in your testimony. You have more work to do in yourself to be truly remorseful about what you have done. Go back to jail. When you have processed it more and can acknowledge your role, come back to us. We will hear you for another trial."

The man was stunned by this decision, and so was I. He had recited the facts accurately, as he was supposed to, but the council understood that he did not yet feel truly sorry for his actions. He was not sincerely seeking forgiveness; he just wanted to be pardoned and set free. The council members courageously followed their hearts and stood with their principles. Their decision made a strong statement: only *true* remorse could bring reconciliation and healing to this community. It wasn't enough for this man to follow the script—he had to understand the impact of his actions and truly want to be forgiven.

Up until that day, forgiveness, healing, and reconciliation had been concepts to me. I believed in them, but I had never lived them or put myself on the line in any personal way. I did not understand what it meant to be a victim witnessing an aggressor admitting his crime, like the Tutsi mother who faced her son's killer. I had not understood what it meant to be the criminal standing in front of his community, in front of everyone he grew up with and lived beside, admitting to the terrible things he had done.

That day, I saw how much truth matters. People feel it. Hearts close when truth is not heard, but they open in its presence. Perpetrators have a chance of being truly integrated back into their communities again only when they own their actions from a place of authenticity. This way, they release themselves from the burden of guilt and have a chance to get at the root of whatever pain motivated them in the first place. Surviving victims have a chance of finding peace only when they hear authentic remorse from those who have hurt them. Then they can free themselves from the burden of pain, anger, and resentment toward their aggressors. Reconciliation and forgiveness need to be genuine to be effective.

This is how the quest for truth moves from the distant to the near, from the political to the personal, from something that happens to other people to something that we need to reckon with in our own hearts, in our own lives, and in our own communities.

Intellectually, I knew that seeking forgiveness and reconciliation, even on a personal level, was essential for finding peace in myself. How could I ever talk about forgiveness and healing for the world—between Tutsi and Hutu in Rwanda, between Kurds and Arabs in Iraq, between Christians and Muslims in Nigeria, in all the countries where I was working—if I didn't know their meaning in my heart? How could I repeat Nelson Mandela's phrases of forgiveness in my speeches if I had not truly and authentically forgiven those who had wronged me? What's more, how could I ask for forgiveness from those I had hurt when I had never forgiven myself?

I had to begin with what was closest to me—my broken heart.

*

I had met Saeed a few years after my marriage ended. We were both interested in personal development, obsessed with similar books and life coaches, and wanted to find what we called "the team," a group of like-minded and like-hearted people who could act as our spiritual support network. We met at a social event hosted by a friend from one of these self-development retreats. Because on these retreats participants work through personal issues in the presence of a community, people tend to bond quickly. Friendships develop as people witness one another's pain. I trusted the friendships I had developed in these settings with all my heart. I trusted the space that held these gatherings, the integrity of everyone's willingness to dive into their work, and the honesty and vulnerability of the stories that we all shared.

At the cocktail party, I spent most of my time around my friends, enjoying the wine, hors d'oeuvres, and dance music. But I couldn't help but notice a very attractive man who didn't seem to know many people there. At first, I was too shy to approach him. He looked like Michelangelo's *David* with his very trim body, twinkling eyes, and beautiful smile. Eventually, with the help of a friend, I found the courage to speak to him. He was gentle in his conversation, and I was taken by some of what he shared about his own childhood.

I stayed in touch with Saeed, and one day, when I was giving a party, I mustered my courage to invite him. Not only did he accept, he also sat next to me almost the entire night, making me think that the admiration might be mutual. My heart sparkled with excitement.

As I let Saeed more into my heart, our friendship began to deepen into a romance. Whenever we were together, we talked and laughed nonstop. We hiked in the woods of upstate New York and swam in lakes we encountered on our hikes. He cooked delicious meals for me, from his grandmother's chicken soup recipe to rice dishes that reminded me of home. He admired and supported my dedication to women's rights. When I had to put in long hours at work, he would tell me, "Go make the world better; I will always be here for you." His work was in making art. I admired it and appreciated how it was so different from what I did. In no time, we were falling in love. He would pound his chest and say, "I will always love you. I will always be loyal to you. I will always protect you. I will never lie to you."

Saeed was everything I wanted, but at first I was afraid that he was too good to be true. Were his endearments and expressions of love sincere? Was I seeing all of him, or was I blinded by his handsome face and tender words? My gut instinct told me to be careful, but eventually, after hearing his charming words often enough, I allowed myself to soften. My desire to be loved, to feel safe and protected, won out. He'd smile that gorgeous smile just for me, and I would feel confident that he meant what he said.

Things were wonderful for a while. I introduced Saeed to my friends and my family. I took him to work events and galas, no longer the solo strong woman without a date. Saeed lightened the weight of walking alone. But within a year things started to change. Saeed began to tell little lies. He said he had been at an event with my friends when my friends said they had been somewhere else. He insisted that he had paid for my birthday dinner when in reality my brother had. I let these things pass; I didn't want to make a big deal out of them. Then, Saeed started to distort more personal issues. He would criticize my cooking and my taste in clothes and furniture. These comments hurt, but when I got upset, he'd quickly soothe me and become loving again: "You know I love you. I didn't mean to hurt you. I am so sorry, so sorry." He would say the words enough that I would let the incidents go.

When his criticisms became more frequent, I started to doubt my every move. I could not yet see that his behavior was abusive. I got tired of resisting his little attacks and just gave in to the pattern of criticism followed by love. Sometimes I thought he might be right. Maybe I was not a good cook. Maybe my fashion sense was poor. After all, it was true that I had gained a pound or two. Other times I knew he was wrong, but I didn't press the issue because I didn't want to fight.

My friends had not noticed anything strange about him, which made me doubt myself more. Instead, I started getting upset at him for the smallest things—if he didn't smile when he saw me or call me back right away. Without understanding why, I would cry without any provocation, bursting into tears at home, at work, in hotel rooms, wherever I was. When I would come to my senses momentarily, I'd tell Saeed that if he kept criticizing me, I would leave. Then he'd cry and beg me to stay. "But I love you so much, Zainab!" So I stayed, although he'd soon be badgering me again.

This continued until one day I looked at myself in the mirror and said, "This is not who I am." I couldn't point to what exactly was happening; I just felt like I was losing myself. I worked up my courage to face Saeed.

"I still love you, even though you're hurting me," I told him. "Please tell me the truth. Is there something that I need to know? Are you having money problems? Health issues? Is it something in your family? Is there another woman?"

I begged him for the truth. At least if I understood what was in his heart, I could understand, in a bigger sense, what was happening to us and to me. We had both committed to living in truth, after all. Saeed stayed silent. I felt less and less like I was in a loving relationship based on trust and more like I was playing three-card monte with a savvy street hustler.

After a couple more months of confusion and painful self-doubt, I realized that it was time to take a final stand. I had to extricate myself from this unhealthy dynamic.

"I don't understand what is going on," I told him as we sat on my orange sofa in my home. "At this point, you are abusing me. I wish you would just tell me the truth, whatever it is. You are pulling me in and then pushing me away. I've reached my limit. If you can't tell me what is going on, then you need to leave my life immediately. I cannot accept this treatment. The day you can communicate truthfully what's going on, I will listen. Until then, you need to go."

Saeed was not a talker, and that day, too, he stayed silent. I had taken my stand. I had given him an opportunity to embody the values he said he followed and to save our relationship. It was all up to him now. With a flight to catch, I said good-bye.

In that moment, I took ownership of myself, but it didn't stop the tears or the pain. I still did not understand the reasons for Saeed's behavior. I missed him. I doubted my decision even as I stood firm in it. Two months later, I got my answer. An acquaintance from our self-development and spiritual retreats called me: "Zainab, I owe you an apology. I saw Saeed with another woman while he was still with you. They denied that there was anything between them, but I kept seeing them together, and eventually I caught them kissing. I'm so sorry for not telling you earlier—I thought you should at least know now."

The truth was that Saeed had been with another woman for many months before I stood up for myself. Instead of having the courage to tell me about his affair, he just criticized me and made me feel bad about myself. Who knows how long the charade would have lasted if I hadn't taken a stand?

Beyond Saeed's affair, I was devastated by the circle of friends who had known about it and said nothing: not to Saeed, not to me, and not to the woman he was having the relationship with. If this community that I had so trusted as we did our personal work together—talking about the importance of showing up in honesty about our feelings—could keep such a secret from me, whom could I ever trust?

Someone once told me that betrayal is like a dagger that pierces deep into the heart. The knife goes deeper with those we love and trust because muscles soften in the company of friends. We do not expect the knife from *them*. I was feeling the deep cut of this dagger—and it hurt me to the core. Still, I had a hard time believing that the people we love hurt us out of cruelty. It's more likely that they hurt us from their own place of hurt. Full hearts, secure hearts, do not betray. When we are afraid, insecure, feel powerless or even jealous, we can violate the love and trust that others give to us.

Realizing that Saeed was lying to and betraying himself, I started to wonder if I had ever done the same thing: betrayed myself out of my own insecurity and fear. When had I not stood up for myself? When had I let Saeed—or anyone—tell me who I was? When had I created illusions about the people I loved, thinking they meant well even when they were being cruel? When had I ignored my instincts? When had I known that I was being lied to but said nothing?

It was then, in the midst of my pain, that I first became aware that part of me was still wrapped up in old insecurities and fears. There was still a vulnerable little girl within me who was alive and well, despite the strong woman I'd become as an adult. When we do not heal from our past, we keep unconsciously repeating it until we learn its lessons. In my case, the child part of me wanted to feel loved and safe and was afraid of feeling abandoned and lonely. Whether this came from my childhood and upbringing or not, it was my first time seeing that fearful, anxious girl within me.

Consumed by that fear, I would ignore my instincts and let go of my power so as not to lose someone's love. Even though by then I had been running a hugely successful enterprise and bringing aid and resources to women in desperate straits, instead of standing up for myself, I'd sacrifice myself. If I were nice and loving enough, I thought, I would be safe. Really, I was acting out of insecurity, from a part of me that wanted to please, wanted to be perfect, didn't want to be judged, and, more than anything, wanted to be loved.

It was a doll that helped me nourish and heal this vulnerable child part of me. I was in Mexico City giving a speech about understanding war and peace from a woman's perspective when a young woman, who had come to ask a question, presented me with a traditional Mexican doll as a gift.

"To remember Mexico," she said, handing me a brown wool doll in a white dress. The doll had a baby doll wrapped on her back with a bright, colorful shawl.

I took the doll with a smile and a thank-you without knowing what to do with it or how I was going to fit it into my carry-on luggage. But that night in my hotel room, restless from jet lag, I picked up the doll and I found myself hugging it as I started falling asleep. It was as if the adult me was holding the child version of herself. For the first time, I felt I was actually embracing and loving the child in me and protecting her with all my might.

For women, loving ourselves can seem selfish or self-indulgent. It's much easier to punish ourselves for all the ways we are not perfect. How dare we take care of ourselves first? But there cannot be true healing without love, and that includes self-love. Until then, I had thought self-love meant getting massages, working out, and buying nice clothes. It was something I thought I could get from the world outside myself. Not until I started hugging that doll did I learn to hold myself—by myself and for myself. I learned to listen to the pitch of my voice and the feelings in my body, to my dreams and instincts. They told me which parts of me were the little girl acting out and which were the strong woman who had values and opinions. I was learning how to be my own ally.

When we don't let fear run our lives, we can listen to our better judgments and make different choices. When I attended to my needs and instincts, I could be more present in my dealings with others. To truly understand the giving and receiving of love, I had to take the time to give it to myself—and genuinely receive it.

Eventually, the anger and disappointment I felt toward myself for letting Saeed betray me transformed into acceptance and affection.

I learned to comfort and soothe the little girl in me whose perspective had been running my intimate life for such a long time. From there, I saw Saeed's betrayal in a different light, too. I could see more clearly that there was a hurt child in him as well who had motivated him to betray me. Maybe love happened only in stolen moments for Saeed. Maybe that was the unresolved wound that was driving him. Realizing this, my anger and hurt began to dissolve. I found compassion for the insecure parts of him, just as I had found compassion for the insecure parts of me. The more I could understand and forgive the part of *me* that had betrayed me, the more I could understand and forgive the part of him that had betrayed me—and himself.

Practicing forgiveness is a multifaceted process. First we have to learn how to forgive ourselves so that we can let go of the burden of painful guilt. It is the deepest act of kindness toward ourselves. From there, we have the capacity to forgive others. We can see that those who have hurt us are driven by something they are not in control of either. When we forgive them, they no longer control our story. Forgiving is like taking a step toward our own freedom. From there it becomes possible to identify whom we have hurt ourselves, which is a very humbling and even scary experience.

It was one thing to observe the process of forgiveness in the gacaca courts in Rwanda, where I saw several killers offer remorse and ask for pardon, and quite another thing for me to stand in front of the friends and family I had hurt and ask for their forgiveness. This part of the process was an exercise in vulnerability. Yet exposing myself completely was the only way I knew to fully embody the meaning of forgiveness. It was an act of humility, and it required a lot of courage.

I did not come up with this idea myself. It was a former colleague, Samantha, who sought me out years after I had left Women for Women International. She taught me, by example, what it feels like to initiate a conversation of forgiveness. We hadn't been close when we worked together. In fact, although it had remained polite, our relationship had become distant and silent toward the end of my tenure. So I was surprised when Samantha asked to meet up for coffee. At first, I said of course, whenever she was in New York I'd be happy to meet with her. But Samantha wanted to nail down a time and a place where we could meet. She would come from her home in Washington, DC, just for our meeting. Her persistence made me think that she might need a recommendation letter or some help finding work, so I agreed, and we made the necessary arrangements.

I met Samantha in my favorite coffee shop, right below my apartment. I dressed casually, in jeans and a sweater, but Samantha arrived wearing a crisp blue fitted shirt, her hair freshly done, as if she were attending a business meeting. The waitstaff took our orders for coffee as we settled in. At first, we circled the unspoken issue by catching up on our families, my work, and all the usual chitchat.

"Oh yes, yes, everyone is doing great," Samantha said, giving me a ten-minute description of her kids' personalities and school lives and an even longer explanation of how her husband's business was expanding. Finally, half an hour later, my cappuccino was finished, and I was getting impatient with our dance of words. In a moment of awkward silence, I jumped at the chance to be direct.

"So, Samantha, is there anything I can do for you? Do you need a recommendation for a job or something?"

"No, nothing like that," she said, looking down and clearing her throat. "I am here to ask for your forgiveness. When we worked together, I really, really wanted your job. So I bad-mouthed you. I spoke badly about you in front of some colleagues. I've realized that I was destructive and that it came out of my desire to have your job. So I want to apologize for backstabbing you."

In my initial shock, I tried to wash over the topic and move on to something less serious. "Well, that happened years ago," I said lightly. "And it was not the reason I left the organization anyway."

"That doesn't mean that I don't need to apologize," she insisted, her eyes meeting mine. I could see embarrassment in them mixed with courage. She looked down into the bottom of her empty espresso cup as if gathering her strength to face me one more time. Then she looked up. "I am here today to ask you for forgiveness. Just that. Will you give it to me?"

Truth be told, there were moments in the years of my work with Samantha when I did feel a tension and animosity between us, but my irritation had been fleeting. I had not forgotten these incidents; I'd just decided to let them be. I hadn't even mentioned them to anyone else.

As her request sank in, it felt like she was giving me the mother of all gifts—her truth. It softened the stiffness in our conversation, and my whole attitude toward her shifted. Moved and inspired by her courage, I gave Samantha my forgiveness and thanked her for showing up in this way. Then, I wanted to know more.

"Why are you bringing this up now, Samantha? It was such a long time ago."

"I needed to acknowledge what I had done so that I can move on. My guilt has been holding me back. I want to be in integrity with you, so I need to relieve myself of this burden."

In the past, Samantha had acted from her insecurity, fear, jealousy—whatever it was that was playing in her shadow. In the present, she had the courage to acknowledge her wrongdoing to herself and then ask for forgiveness even when not prompted or required to. In this way, Samantha became a teacher to me. She showed up with full integrity, no matter how hard it was to sit in that chair and ask for forgiveness. She must not have expected any reward other than knowing that she was facing up to her less-than-noble actions.

When we hugged good-bye that afternoon in the coffee shop, Samantha had my deepest gratitude and respect. She had released me from my lingering suspicions of her and of that time in my career. She had freed us both with the truth.

I decided to take this gift Samantha had offered me and pay it forward. I had people to apologize to. The foremost of them was Amjad, my kind ex-husband, who had shown so much love and respect throughout our fourteen years of marriage. During our early years, when I was growing into myself, I could be very fearful and insecure. My inability to be fully truthful with myself or with others sometimes made me act out. Although we had divorced amicably and were still friends, it was no longer enough for me to leave things unacknowledged. I wanted to own the actions that I'd always suspected had hurt him.

I asked Amjad to have coffee with me on one of his business trips to New York. When he finally managed to steal time away, we met at the same coffee shop below my apartment where Samantha and I had met a few months earlier.

As I waited for him to arrive, I kept the image of Samantha at the forefront of my mind. Sitting in her seat, I understood even better the vulnerability of that position, that look of courage and embarrassment mixed together. As my hands trembled, I thought of Samantha's trembling hands. As my voice caught in my throat, I remembered her voice cracking as she apologized.

Finally, Amjad sat in front of me.

"How is life treating you?" he asked, kissing me hello on the cheek.

"Very well. No complaints. How is your wife doing?"

We went back and forth in the dance of questions and niceties, ordering some food and catching up on the light stuff.

Finally, I looked at Amjad directly: "I asked you to come because I need to apologize. I know I acted cruelly toward you at times during our marriage. I could be harsh with you, and sometimes I deliberately ignored you. I know I didn't pay attention when you were trying to tell me important things about your past or when you asked for help with your work—and I could have helped you."

Amjad let me speak. At first, I spoke in general terms. Then, I worked up my courage and got more detailed in my stories. That's when he stopped me. "Zainab, this all happened a long time ago. It's been nine years since our divorce."

"I know that. But I still need to apologize. I owe it to you and to our friendship. I'm sorry. I am really sorry for how I behaved at the end of our marriage. Today, I am asking for your forgiveness. "

It didn't feel right to sweep all the slights and omissions and little acts of cruelty from our relationship under the rug. I knew they had hurt Amjad, and I knew that I had been responsible for that hurt. I needed to shake out that rug and clean it until its dust disappeared into clear air so that our loving friendship could continue to evolve.

When I had said everything I needed to say, Amjad looked at me with his kind eyes. "It's all good, Zainab. I have my own list of things to apologize to you for, too. We both had our share of mistakes that contributed to the end of our relationship."

We talked about our past, what I did and what he did, what I didn't do and what he didn't do. I told him all about Samantha and Saeed and how I was learning to give and receive love and forgiveness in my life. Patient and gracious as ever, Amjad listened to everything. Then, together, we blessed our past and let it go.

Not until the moment I sat in front of Amjad did I realize how hard it is to apologize without making any excuses for my actions. There were many justifications I could have offered for my offenses and mistakes, but really a genuine apology was all that was required. It is easy to be the victim, to be the one who was wronged. We prefer to see ourselves as good and above blame, but it's never the whole story. It is much harder to admit that sometimes we are also the villain. That we are human, and so we are all flawed.

Expressing our guilt and remorse with sincerity and humility means acknowledging how small we are in this vast universe. For a moment, we accept that we are as tiny as a particle of dust and no more powerful than a fly. It is the most humbling experience. Yet these moments help us to take a different view of ourselves than the usual one. In many ways, these moments show our connectedness to each other as individuals. We are all the same in our moments of pain and in our moments of humility. Seeing this reminds us to try our best to live this life we are given. It gives us compassion for anyone who is going through life's exhilarating ups and inevitable downs. We've all been there.

I never knew if Saeed was aware of how much pain he had caused me. Today, it doesn't matter. Forgiving him—without him asking for my forgiveness—was my gift to myself. That process shed new light into my own darkness, calmed my spirit, and gave me a better sense of self. It allowed me to feel more love for the woman I am and for the child who still lives within me.

Twenty years since experiencing one of the most horrific genocides in modern times, Rwanda has become one of the most prosperous countries in Africa. In thousands of communities, Hutu and Tutsi work side by side farming the land and reconstructing the country. The gacaca court helped neighbors to live beside neighbors again, for mothers to forgive killers, and for rapists to ask for heartfelt pardon. Although no one in Rwanda can ever forget, through forgiveness most Rwandans are working together for themselves and for generations to come.

It takes courage to tell the truth as it is. Sometimes that truth telling will require revealing the most insecure, frightened aspects of ourselves. For me, learning about and learning to practice forgiveness was ultimately a journey of love. I came to realize that not only is it possible to forgive without being asked for forgiveness, it is possible even to love those who betrayed me.

If we see those who betrayed us as we see ourselves, in their fullness and their weakness, we can love both parts of them: the insecure part of them that led them to betrayal and the full part of them that extends its love. May we forgive without being asked for forgiveness. That is the journey of true love.

7

Surrendering Control

Walk humbly on this earth so you may
hear your heart's call and the call of the divine.

In our efforts to secure the happiness, the love, and even the spiritual connection we desire, we often try to control our experiences. We truly believe that this will get us what we want. At first, our scripts—how we think things are supposed to go—set us in motion and give us a direction to go in. But if, over time, these scripts become a rigid set of expectations, then they imprison us. They become our Achilles' heels. Trapped in our ideas about how life needs to be, we often find ourselves disappointed when it does not measure up. We berate ourselves for not achieving our dreams and goals exactly as we imagined them. At the same time, we may be overlooking both the beauty and the opportunities that are right in front of us. We don't see them because they weren't a part of our plan.

Controlling every aspect of our lives can have the opposite effect of what we want. Instead of making us happy, it has the potential to stop us from living life fully. It can prevent the ambitious entrepreneur from experiencing everyday joys while she works hard to build her business. It can interfere with parents' ability to experience of the joy of raising children as they navigate all the inevitable challenges. It can stop the person who craves a true connection with a higher consciousness from fully connecting to the divine from his own heart.

Behind our attempts to control life lie our fears. We fear failing, being hurt, being judged, not succeeding, being humiliated. We're afraid not to feel loved, accepted, and, ultimately, happy. But there *is* another way to achieve these things. We can show up in our lives, set our intentions, do our work, and then *let go* of our attachments to what happens next. We can make all the necessary effort to get what we want by planning well, working hard, getting the right experience, and even buying the right clothes—but then we let what happens happen.

When we allow life to breathe in and out of us, instead of trying to make the world conform to our expectations, then our lives have a chance of becoming an incredible journey full of unimaginable surprises. We have a chance to relax into whatever life brings. It is another way of describing *surrender*.

Surrender is not a popular word in our high-pressure world. It can seem hard to understand. How can *letting go* of what we really, truly want lead us to more achievements, more success, respect, recognition, and love? It seems illogical. But showing up in our lives, walking in our truth, and then letting go of our expectations create the very path that takes us to freedom. A teacher once told me surrender is about letting go of attachments to outcome. It is like walking in step with the actual rhythm of earth, at a pace far slower than our usual one and in a silence far more silent than our minds. If we want to explore and experience life more fully and authentically and be open to opportunities that we could never have dreamed up on our own, then surrender is what we need to do.

Elliot, an athlete, won the prestigious trophy he wanted by practicing surrender. His goal was to lead his university rowing team to win the Harvard-Yale Regatta, an annual boat race between two rival universities. Elliott loved to row, and he was ultimately aiming to earn a place on the US national team. It was a big dream and required a huge commitment. He woke up early every day, six days a week, to do three hours of practice in the morning, and then he ran and did strength training in the afternoon. He ate the right foods, and he got the necessary sleep. It was only his first year of college, but he was very competitive: if his coach required the team to do two courses of training, Elliot did three. Working this hard, he became captain of his crew, the one who set the speed and rhythm for the whole team.

When the day of the race arrived, Elliot felt prepared. But right from the starting gun, his team fell behind. They couldn't close the gap. The coach was screaming at them, and Elliot was calling out a faster time, but they couldn't row fast enough. Stressed and agitated, some of his rowers were even throwing up under the pressure. The boats in front kept getting farther ahead. Finally came the moment of surrender.

"I was so tense that at one point I decided to close my eyes and just take a moment to breathe," Elliot told me. "I got quiet. I let myself feel the breeze against my face and the force of the water under the boat. I just listened to the sounds around me. Suddenly, I didn't need to push as hard. I let go and worked with the rhythm of the water."

As Elliot called the stroke again from this place of inner tranquility, his team started to come up from behind. They were gaining speed and passing other boats. Tuned in to an inner rhythm, one that had nothing to do with competing, Elliot led his team to win the race.

The moment Elliot let go of his focus on winning, he surrendered. When he synched his breath and movement with the water beneath him, he let himself feel the experience fully rather than only pushing aggressively to the finish line. He did everything he could do—set his intention, made the commitment, exceeded the training requirements, prepared his mind and his breath. But the secret to winning was the last thing he could have imagined. The secret was to just *be*, to live fully inside that moment. In that surrender he found his victory.

Of course, victory is hardly guaranteed. Nor is it always the path to happiness. There is a verse in the Qur'an that says, "And it may be that you dislike a thing which is good for you." I take this to mean that our misfortunes can also lead to our fortunes. Things do not always go the way we expect or plan for, yet that does not mean that they are ultimately bad for us. The difficult things that I have experienced in life—abuse, poverty, failure, and loss—have each led me to a new love, new joy, new gains, and new, better ways of living. If I'd seen them only as bad, because I disliked them in the moment they were happening, I would have missed the treasures they contained.

When we surrender our firm ideas of what things *should* be, other options arise. That doesn't mean it's easy. For much of my life, I did not allow myself to experience surrender because I was busy trying to achieve and accomplish. I wanted to ensure good outcomes in my work, in love, in family, and everything I did. In the process, I tried to control as many aspects of my life as I could. I thought that was the best—and the only—way forward. I wanted my humanitarian and media projects to succeed, so I monitored every discussion and decision: the small, the medium, and the large ones. I feared being hurt in relationships, so I scrutinized each person I dated thoroughly. I would overanalyze his personality and actions to make sure that I saw no danger signs. Was he in touch enough? Did he cook me dinner and remember my favorite foods? Did he surprise me with nice things like flowers and my favorite chocolate cake? Did he call enough while he was traveling?

The need to control seemed to guarantee my success and my safety. So when I got the opportunity to visit the holy city of Mecca in Saudi Arabia, a country I feared, I wanted to control every aspect of that experience, too. It was during this trip that I learned the true meaning of surrender.

For many years I would not even consider setting foot in Saudi Arabia. It was a conservative Muslim country whose strict interpretation of Islamic laws frightened me. The country's "moral police," when they were in effect, enforced a narrow interpretation of Islam in people's everyday lives. In Saudi Arabia, a lot of normal behaviors were prescribed, including what people (especially women) could wear, how people should pray, and how men and women could interact. When the moral police detected an infraction, they did not hesitate to confront it in public. I had read many news stories of women at the mall or walking on the streets being hit or even whipped for an ankle too exposed or a veil not pulled down far enough. As a woman, I resisted going to a country where my basic rights would not be protected, where I wasn't allowed to drive, and where I could not dress or move freely.

In the spring of 2016, when the Massachusetts Institute of Technology invited me to Saudi Arabia to give the keynote address at a conference for young Arab men and women on innovation in the Arab world, I decided to put my fears aside. If my goal was to live a life of love, not of fear, then I needed to confront this particular fear. I decided to take the opportunity presented to me.

I expected Saudi Arabia to be harsh and oppressive, but to my surprise, it was a beautiful and gracious country. I arrived in Jeddah, a port city on the Red Sea, where the country's unforgiving desert was broken by clusters of tall palm trees and the deep blue of the vast sea waters. Jeddah was a mix of charming, narrow old streets and contemporary skyscrapers, modern cafés, and museums. It was an elegant oasis.

The people surprised me, too. I had been nervous on the plane. What if I couldn't wear the required clothes properly? When the airport staff saw me struggling to put on the long, black linen abya that women were required to wear, they assured me that I did not have to wear it perfectly. I could drape the chiffon head scarf over my shoulders instead of covering every inch of my head. When I put it on, it actually felt easy and elegant—not what I had been expecting. As I walked into the airport, a welcoming party of students and conference presenters greeted me. They took me around to restaurants and cafés in Jeddah, proudly showing me their city. In all the public places we went, I was surprised to see women and men sitting and eating together, smoking the traditional flavored tobacco called *shisha* from glass-bottomed water pipes. They looked relaxed and comfortable together. All of these scenes and experiences were contrary to my expectations and stereotypes of Saudi Arabia.

My new young friends were students and young entrepreneurs from all over the Middle East, and our conversation ranged widely. We talked about love and relationships, art and entrepreneurial ambitions, and I heard their social commentaries on the state of reform in Saudi Arabia. Saudi Arabian culture was an anomaly in the Middle East. Instead of becoming more progressive as it grew wealthy from oil over the past several decades, it had become more closed, ruled by Wahhabi traditions. The Wahhabis are a sect of Muslims who subscribe to a literal way of implementing religion in daily life. Under Wahhabis, Islam in Saudi Arabia went from being a religion practiced in a way that was individually oriented and made to fit modern realities to one that was tribally oriented, strict, and rigid in its application. The rights of women particularly became very restricted. How Islam was practiced, too, was closely monitored by the state.

"I know there are lots of issues with my country," said Hend, a young Saudi woman with curly hair and a beautiful dimple on her right cheek. She had studied business and communications at Harvard. "My friends and I, along with many other people, are pushing for change. It is just hard for me to be a part of the mass criticism of Saudi Arabia from the outside. After all, it is my country, and I love it. So, for me, it is easier to push from within."

The good, the bad, and the ugly exist everywhere, I reminded myself, *even in the most powerful and most conservative country in the Muslim world.* This young Saudi woman saw how her country was beautiful in its strong family ties, love for poetry, subtle humor, and generosity toward others. She also saw how it was like a heavy anchor with its extreme values within Islam that kept her and the rest of the Muslim world—which was sometimes influenced by Saudi money—from moving forward. Her love motivated her to try to improve her country rather than to abandon it, in spite of the real restrictions it imposed on her life.

Meeting Hend and the other conference participants helped to humanize Saudi Arabia for me. I had been so attached to my own preconceived idea of the country as oppressive that I had not been able to see beyond that idea, to really see its people and the beauty of its culture. My political concerns about Saudi Arabia's impact on the larger Muslim world did not vanish during this visit, but now I had a larger, more complex view of it. By deciding to look my own fear in the eyes and not let myself be controlled by it, I was able to see the fuller story. I had to see past my rigid ideas first.

During the conference itself, I met many young women and men who were passionate about their social or business enterprise. It was inspiring to see humor, compassion, and forward thinking in action. An Egyptian woman presented a nonelectric water-distribution system for farmers in remote areas; a Jordanian man showed how he manufactured affordable prosthetics for crippled refugees. There was even a karaoke machine in Arabic, designed by a Lebanese attendee.

Over the course of many conversations that weekend, I learned that Mecca, the holy site, was only an hour from where I was staying in King Abdullah Economic City. I hadn't realized I was so close. At this point in my life, I was very interested in exploring the meaning of God in any context, practicing what my mother had always told me: to make sure I looked in all directions, because God was everywhere. I decided I could not be so close to Mecca and not go. It was right there in front of me, and I was curious.

The sacred journey to Mecca is one of the major tenets in Islam. But since I grew up in a secular Muslim family, not a religious one, fulfilling these tenets was never a priority for me. For us, Islam was mostly a part of our culture and everyday life. That meant we didn't eat pork, we fasted during the month of Ramadan, and we celebrated regular Islamic holidays, just like everyone around us. Praying five times a day or worshiping at the mosque or doing a pilgrimage was not part of my family's life. How we lived was quite normal throughout the Muslim world and still is today. We viewed religious practice as a private matter to be decided between each individual and God. Even as my parents became more observant in their later years, they never frowned on my less observant ways.

Although I grew up in a nonobservant family, my heart often responded to the call of the divine. As a child, I felt a connection to a higher consciousness. I would sometimes cry with an overwhelming sense of awe and love when I heard the call to prayer echoing through Baghdad's skies or heard the word "God" pronounced with devotion. But I resisted fully embracing my native Islam because, as with any institutionalized religion, the rules, dogma, and rituals that accompanied it seemed too oppressive and strict. They didn't seem to allow for a connection to what was truly divine.

I had long explored other spiritual traditions, though, such as those of Native Americans, indigenous cultures of South America, and various schools of Buddhism. My lack of attachment to these traditions allowed me to connect more openheartedly to their philosophies of life and to observe their customs and movements in ways that I would have rejected in my own tradition. As of today, I've probably prayed more in sweat lodges and Buddhist temples than I have ever prayed in Islamic mosques.

When I first heard a First Nations medicine woman, Virginia, from the Anishinabe in eastern Canada, talk about the importance of rituals, I recoiled from the idea. I wanted to escape rituals, not participate in new ones. But remembering how my mother had always told me to seek God in the trees, in the earth, and in the air I breathed, over time the Native American ways felt natural and freeing. I was able to listen to Virginia and accept her wisdom. I learned to fast, build a cedar floor, and collect the wood needed for our sweat lodge ceremonies. I became more open to understanding her tradition, and in time, that led me full circle, back to understanding and experiencing my own tradition in a deeper, more authentic way.

Truth be told, I was still nervous to visit Mecca, despite my wonderful, welcoming experience at the conference. I still dreaded fanatic clerks or police who might reprimand me for not covering myself or behaving properly. These fears were so strong in my mind that even though I was not required to cover my hair in the places I had visited so far, I still feared being yelled at or worse. But I decided I was not going to let my fear get in my way. I wanted to experience the holy place that millions of Muslims all over the world bow to every day as they make their prayers. I wanted to experience that sacred site myself.

"Not to worry," said a Saudi princess who was also speaking at the conference. We'd met at a lunch given for some of the participants. She was hard to miss in her Louis Vuitton shoes and impeccable makeup. When she heard of my hesitations to visit Mecca, she immediately offered to help. "It is a most beautiful experience," she said in her fluent British English. "I go there all the time. The best time to go is at dawn, when the weather is still beautiful. When you are ready, I will arrange for a personal driver and guide for you. It is part of my hospitality for you as a guest in my country. You will be all right, my dear."

I was relieved. Having this escort would help me avoid the huge crowds and protect me from the moral police, I thought. Two mornings later, I woke up at 5 a.m. and did my ablutions, washing my hands, feet, face, and hair. I prayed in the traditional Islamic way that I recalled from my grade-school in Baghdad: "Please, God, direct me to the right path." I dressed and put the black linen abya on top of my clothes and the black chiffon head scarf over my head.

A driver met me at my hotel lobby in King Abdullah Economic City to take me to Mecca. As we drove, we heard the traditional Muslim call to prayer, the *adhan*, echoing through the skies. It was like a song reminding us of the presence of the divine. I rolled down the car window to let in the holy sounds along with the morning desert breeze. My heart tingled with excitement and still a little bit of fear.

Things went smoothly until we arrived in Mecca and discovered that all the roads near the mosque were closed. Cars could not get close to drop off passengers. Crowds were already forming, and it seemed like thousands of people were filling the streets. I had no idea how far we were from the Kaaba, the House of God, where the pilgrimage officially took place. A mile? Two miles? Three?

"Ma'am, all the roads are closed," said my driver, his Arabic tinged with a Pakistani accent. "Do you want to walk? Or should I keep trying?"

"Let's see if there is another street open," I said. Another forty minutes passed. The driver asked the same question, and I gave the same answer. Finally, it was clear that I had to either give up and go back to the hotel or get out of the car and walk into the sea of people.

I worry about walking in massive crowds anywhere in the world. I get overwhelmed, nervous, claustrophobic. In this situation, as a single woman in a foreign country without a guide to help me find my way, I felt even more anxious. It added to my preexisting fear of being confronted.

I had to make a decision. With great hesitation, I said good-bye to my driver, got out of the car, and entered the crowd. I trusted that once I found my guide near the main doors of the Kaaba, I would feel safe.

Even on foot, it was no easy journey. The weather was already hot and muggy. I walked and walked, jostled among people of all nationalities, all colors, races, and ethnicities. After more than half an hour of walking, we reached the main gate. Now I would find my guide. But as I searched my purse, I couldn't find his cell number—to my dismay, I realized that I'd left it with the driver. I would have to ask around to find where the guides gathered.

The first person I asked sent me in one direction. The next person I asked sent me in another direction. I walked back and forth from one point to the other, searching for my guide. I wasn't getting anywhere.

Why was this happening? Why would all the doors to the pilgrimage close in my face? I had come with excitement and an open heart. I had overcome my fears and my prejudices and was eager to make amends with my own spiritual tradition. I even had the perfect VIP plan to protect me! Yet nothing was budging. I wasn't getting the experience I wanted.

Holding back my tears, I finally approached a policeman. His uniform was the one I had feared and judged from afar for years. Yet in that moment, I had no choice but to ask him for help.

"I am lost, and I can't find my guide," I said, clinging to my purse. My face felt twisted up in frustration. "Can you help me?"

"I can tell you where the guides are," he said in a gentle voice. "But you seem so frustrated that I feel no matter what I say, you won't believe me."

I went silent. He clearly saw my anxiety.

"In any case, why do you want a guide? You can do the visit on your own."

"I don't know how!" I said, wanting to cry. With my exclamation, he met my eyes. I was astonished. In Saudi Arabian culture, women and men who are not related are not supposed look each other in the eyes. This man didn't hesitate to. In that moment, I saw what kind eyes he had.

"Are you alone?" he asked gently. He knew I needed a companion on such an important journey, even though it was okay for me to visit the House of God by myself. In the heart of Islam, women and men walk side by side, without division. They are equal in front of God.

"Yes, I am alone," I said. "And I am scared of being yelled at for doing something wrong. I don't want anyone to bother me in my moment of worship." I raised my hands and dropped them by my sides, making the linen fabric of my black abya ripple in the air.

"It's easy. Come, I will show you. You will get more blessings this way. First you go down to the Kaaba—the huge black cube. Walk around it seven times counterclockwise. After the seventh time, leave the circle and make a prayer to give thanks to God. From there, go to the Safa and Marwah, two small hills inside the compound, where you walk in commemoration of Hajar, wife of the prophet Ibrahim.

Walk between the two big rocks seven times—you can run, too—and on the seventh time stop and cut a piece of your hair as a sacrifice. That's how you do it."

I thanked him and turned to look in the direction he was pointing. In truth, though, I was still frustrated, afraid, and confused.

"You *can* do it," he continued, sensing my anxiety. "But if you still want the guide, I will show you where to find one."

"No, no. I am going to follow your instructions." To my surprise, I trusted the policeman. "Thank you, again. So much."

I turned away with a sliver of courage and walked back into the crowd. I was immediately swallowed up and carried forward by the surging masses. Just as I was finding some calm in myself, the call to prayer sounded again. When this happens, no one is allowed to enter the compound. Doors close to prepare for prayers. To me it seemed as if yet another door was closing in my face. We would have to wait until the prayers were concluded to continue forward. I burst into tears. This really wasn't working.

Trapped among my fellow pilgrims, I could not go forward, nor, in that moment, could I go back. Tears staining my face, I looked around me. I saw hundreds of thousands of people from all over the world: Arabs, Pakistanis, Chinese, Americans, Africans, Indians, and all other kinds of Muslims. The men were wrapped in *Ihram*, a white unhemmed cotton sheet, and the women in black abyas. We were like a beautiful mass of black-and-white human ribbons. I could see the Kaaba right there in front of us. Seeing what others were doing, I found a place to sit down on the cold marble floor of the courtyard. I leaned against a giant white marble column engraved with prayers and took out a copy of the Qur'an, the holy book of Islam, that some-one had given me earlier in my trek. I opened it and started reading.

The Qur'an is considered the miracle of Prophet Muhammad, an illiterate man who spoke a complex, poetic language. His words are thought of as direct revelations of God, addressing everything from astronomy and law to spirituality and history. Even though Arabic is my native language, I don't always understand the Qur'an's zigzagging discourse and have never succeeded in reading the text all the way to the end. The Qur'an is like an erratic wind that blows from kindness and spiritual love to harshness and earthly rules. It is like a concert of notes that go up and down the scales of the material and spiritual realms. One set of notes elevates us with its powerful love, while another frightens us with its strictness. I love the verses on love, mercy, and kindness, as well as the passages on the equality of women and men in front of God. But the Qur'an's passages on punishments and hardships for disbelievers are hard to comprehend. How could God command things that felt so rigid and harsh? I could never get through those parts.

When taken in the right spirit, contextually rather than literally, the Qur'an creates a beautiful symphony of words and wisdom. God is neither he nor she. God is not birthed nor given birth. God is never only love and never only fear—for God is all. This is most beautifully expressed in the ninety-nine names of God given in the text, each carrying the opposite meaning of each other: God is the merciful and the punisher, the avenger and the forgiver, the expander and the restrainer, the firm one and the kind one, and so on until the hundredth name, which is left unknown. God encompasses all of these feelings and experiences but ultimately exists beyond them.

That day, sitting on the ground in the courtyard, my tears drying, I didn't get very far in reading the Qur'an. No wonder, I thought, there are so many schools of thought in Islam—because there are so many different interpretations of the Qur'an. I closed the book. Right now, I wanted the simplest thing: to connect to God from my heart. I had tried and tried. I had the right clothes, I had the right guidance, I had walked, I had overcome my fear of the moral police, I had given everything I could, and yet all my efforts had failed. I decided to do the only other thing left to do—pray.

"God, I am confused," I said in my heart. "I don't know the meaning of this. I come with an open heart, but the doors to your holy house keep closing. So now I surrender all my plans. I simply surrender."

In that moment, sitting in that sea of humans, my heart calmed down, and my ego quieted. The call to prayer started: "There is no God but one God." *That is the Islam I know*, I thought. It is not divisive, it does not terrorize, it does not treat female citizens as if they are dangerous or paint foreigners and outsiders with suspicion. It is about love, about moving together as one. *This is the Islam everyone needs to experience—that I needed to experience,* I thought, *with the grace of its spiritual traditions, the beauty of its teachings on modesty and kindness.* I realized in that moment that I did not need to be guided or protected to make my full prayers to God.

The voice making the call to prayer intoned a deep longing for God. It inspired us as we sat lined up next to one another on the marble floor in surrender and submission. If I had been a bird flying from above, I would have seen our lines of black and white kneeling in the same moment, all echoing the same prayer, one that I had not done for years since my childhood, and in one voice. Hundreds of thousands of *amens* were said in the same breath as we recited the same words with the same heart. There we were as one, as kings and queens and servants and farmers. There was no class, no race, no gender, no nationality—no separation between those who had and those who did not, those who were learned and those who were not. We were all one in our love, in our longing, and in our submission to the divine. I was nothing but an equal to each and every one of the people around me.

My tears poured out uncontrollably, just as with everyone around me. At the end of the prayer, I turned to my right and thanked the angel on my right shoulder and to my left to thank the angel on my left shoulder, as was part of the custom. I then looked to the person to my right and prayed for her blessings, as she did for me, then turned to the person on my left and did the same for her.

With the prayers done, the doors to the courtyard opened, and we slowly moved to join the crowd going around the large black cube etched with gold in the center of the mosque's square. The crowd was so massive that I had only two choices for how to walk: to stiffen up in my fear of crowds or surrender to the swell of people walking and churning around the Kaaba in slow circles. I decided to surrender. It was the safer option. It was easier to go with the rhythm of bodies moving together in one movement than to resist it.

I looked at all the faces around me in the square. Some looked hip and cool, some looked traditional, and some looked like fundamentalists. Some looked kind, and some looked mean. But there was one clarity: we were all together, and we were all one. We were men and women, shoulder to shoulder, body to body, all walking next to one another, with one another. It's true that some people in the crowd were behaving badly, sitting in the midst of the circling and thus disturbing everyone around them. One young man moved to stop them, but his friend told him to leave them alone, since they didn't know any better. *How beautiful*, I thought. Everyone moved along in unity rather than letting those who were misbehaving take away from the power of the moment. It felt like each one of us was a drop of water in our vast sea of humanity. With that came a breeze of peace that expanded my being with sweet love and humility. My individual ego was nothing before God and nothing amid our collective surging. In that moment, there was no good or bad, no fear or hatred.

I looked up to the sky. All I could hear was silence broken by the longing calls of voices next to me: "Please, God, forgive me!" and "Please, God, have mercy on me!" These voices carried my heart. I joined in and cried for my own forgiveness, for my family's safety and the safety of my friends and loved ones. I cried in my love. I cried as I prayed for peace in my home country and in the world. To my surprise, I cried as I prayed for those who had hurt me so very deeply in my life—people I had thought of as my enemies. I realized then that I thought of my enemies so often, almost every day, that they were becoming close to my heart, like family. In that moment of ecstatic love, I prayed for them, too. We were, everyone, one and equal in front of God.

It was not easy getting out of the massive crowd as I finished the seventh round, but a group of women suddenly surrounded me and helped push me through with them. I sat down to pray my thanks, as the policeman had told me to do. Then came the second part of the ceremony, walking seven times between the two rock formations known as Safa and Marwah. As the policeman had explained to me when I was lost, this was in remembrance of Hajar and her plea for water when she and her son, Ishmael, were abandoned in the desert. Her ardent prayers were answered with water and dates, saving them from certain death. I joined the thousands of feet memorializing her faith as she prayed to survive and the miracle of her deliverance.

Walking in Hajar's footsteps, I started asking for forgiveness for my snobbery. I had been very attached to having a VIP experience of this pilgrimage, and as a result doors had closed in my face. Now, I was thanking God for those obstacles earlier in the day that had forced me to give up my plan. Only by surrendering my attachments to have the luxury and protection of the princess's car and guide did I experience this beauty of moving with everyone and being moved by everyone in what felt like an ocean of love. Doors had opened when I let go and surrendered to the unknown and the mystery of the moment.

In the moment of surrender, all we can do is to observe what surrounds us and see where the moment takes us. It can feel like an eternity between the tension of not knowing how things will work out and the relief of realizing that all is well—between holding our breath and breathing again, between feeling frustrated and feeling at peace. Being present in that moment of the unknown feels like magic. Although the outcome of the experience may not be what we planned for, beyond the moment of surrender there is a reservoir of love that is delicious to experience.

I may have had a unique experience visiting Mecca, but there is nothing unique in the experience of surrender itself. It is available to all. The process moves us from wanting to control a situation, to becoming rigid with frustration, to despairing and giving up our plans, to eventually experiencing the wonder of a completely unexpected outcome, one we never could have imagined for ourselves. We can have this experience all the time if we only observe our moments and truly take in their lessons. Surrender is not a passive thing. It is not about giving up. Nor is it about *not* preparing ourselves for the things and experiences that we want. Surrender teaches us to notice the circle of life. A heartbreak can lead to a new and better love. A death can also bring a new life after it.

A few nights after my pilgrimage experience, I dreamed that I encountered God. I asked, "Were you there at Mecca, God?" The answer was surprising but made sense: *I was not there. The pilgrimage to Kaaba was about getting you all together in one place so you could see one another.*

My pilgrimage to Mecca was a journey, not into the essence of one religion, but into the essence of our human oneness. We fight with each other and among one another, saying, "God only loves *these* people and not *those* people," "My God is better than your God," and so on. But God is already one, undivided. God has no favorites, no resources that will dry up. Like the earth, the divine is about plenty, not scarcity. I do not know what God is in any absolute sense, nor will I ever claim to. My love for the divine is a leap of faith into something I do not understand. But, like the air I breathe, I know it is there, and it is real. By surrendering my fear and my attachments, I had the freedom to experience utter beauty and utter love that I had not known was available to me all along.

What if we allowed ourselves to breathe fully and relax into our strength and expansiveness without thinking, planning, or harboring any rigid expectations of what needs to happen in order to make us happy? What if we lived every aspect of our lives in this state of acceptance and surrender? It is a step toward living in freedom.

Thinking about Virginia and the beautiful indigenous traditions she taught me over the years, it seemed that I had gone all the way around the world just to end up here, in the heart of my hearts, in the beauty that lay at the center of my own native tradition.

8

Freedom Is an Inside Job

We can walk the path of freedom
when we let go of our fears and
dare to be who we truly are.

Throughout this book, I have sought to shine light on the idea that freedom comes from inside, from owning our shadow as well as our light and from walking in our truths in all their complexities. So often, we look to the material world for our ideas of beauty and happiness. We think that a certain dress or car or type of house will bring us the fulfillment we desire. If we live in this kind of neighborhood, or are married to that kind of man, or have a girlfriend with this kind of look, then we'll feel confident. We see gorgeous images of carefree beauty, fame, and effortless success all around us, and we think that we, too, can have the glamour and joy that they promise. But buying into these ideas and images creates an unquenchable desire for more and more things. It's actually fueled by our feelings of scarcity, not by our feelings of well-being. We are embarrassed about what we don't have, and we're afraid that we'll never have it. Then, we try to cover up that shame and worry with more purchases and acquisitions.

The freedom, love, joy, and safety we all desire come only when we find their meaning in our own souls. Freedom is an internal process. No one can do it for us, and no one can sell it to us. Only when we *see* ourselves—truly see ourselves—do we see that beauty is all around us. It is on the *inward* journey that we find the lasting satisfaction we're looking for. Freedom from manipulation, commercialization, and other kinds of judgment and control is an inside job.

For the longest time I did not think I was beautiful. When I was a child, I would watch beauty pageants in awe of all the women who were competing. They had something I would never have: a certain kind of perfection. The Miss Venezuela beauty pageant was one of the best known, broadcasting images of perfect feminine beauty to millions of viewers every year. Even before the contest started, crowds would throng to Caracas, the capital city, where the young contestants practiced and prepared. Screaming fans would wait to catch a glimpse of them, holding up signs of their favorite young women. It was such a scene that bands and circus acts sometimes played. I understood the fans' excitement.

What I didn't know was what these women had to go through to achieve that perfect look. The contestants who were ultimately selected to compete underwent rigorous training. They dieted intensively, received speech, posture, and media training, and were coached to achieve their perfect shape, perfect face, and seductive walk in four-inch heels. They also had operations to adjust their physiques to become truly "perfect."

The perfection of these women's beauty was not natural—it was manufactured. They were beautiful, to be sure, but nature itself never makes things so perfect. The creation of their image begins when they stand before the pageant manager and his team, nearly naked, to have every inch of their faces and bodies scrutinized. What can be improved? What can be made more perfect? The young women become objects to be polished into ideals of feminine beauty.

Anyelika was eighteen years old when she became a finalist for the pageant. Standing in front of the manager and his team in her tiny bikini, she heard the list of surgeries he prescribed: Nose job, breast job, ear job, and a course of steroids to give her a smaller waist. She was sent to the same plastic surgeon all women went to in Caracas. Anyelika was lucky. Other contestants had more surgeries than Anyelika: chin, butt, hips, lips, and so on. No body part was beyond perfecting. Anyelika had seen other women come out looking much worse than they did going in. When she went to the plastic surgeon, she expressed her fear, and he made her a deal: he would only give her a breast enlargement and make some other minor cuts to show the director. Anyelika got away with one surgery. Women who did not protest went through every recommended operation. Anyelika did take the steroids to keep her body weight down, and in the process, her voice changed, her menstrual cycle was disrupted, and she suffered mood swings.

Anyelika didn't win the Miss Venezuela title, but she did go on to compete for Top Model of the World and appear in national campaigns for major brands, continuing her modeling career. Her face was on the cover of fashion magazines all over the world and on billboards in leading international cities. Yet the pressure to stay thin and get more surgeries never went away.

The modeling world, like the world of beauty pageants, had its own dark secrets. Modeling agencies kept girls in debt and underpaid. Predatory photographers preyed on models who were often teenagers from poor families living far from home. Wealthy men who wanted to be seen out on the town with models paid well for their company—and sometimes expected extra favors, too. Many girls were too poor to have their own beds, let alone their own apartments, so they slept together on mattresses squeezed side by side on the floors of crowded rooms. To stay thin, some became bulimic, and others became addicted to drugs. Anyelika took to smoking to curb her appetite. Eventually, she became bulimic herself.

It was her life's dream to become a model, but after years of living on one can of tuna a day, being told by fashion designers that she was just a clothes hanger, and realizing that no one could—or would—protect her from harassment, even when her safety was at risk, Anyelika started to question the price she was paying to realize this dream. She knew that she was luckier than other models. Although she grew up in a humble home, she could always go back to her family. In many cases, the models were too poor to return home. So they became dependent on their work and susceptible to the drugs, the need to succeed, and the abuse of an industry that knew how vulnerable they were. Behind the image of ideal beauty that she projected to the world, there was an ugly system of greed, exploitation, and abuse.

"You should not do things that will harm your person and your soul to achieve your dreams," she told me as she described the modeling world. "There are other ways." No woman's body or soul is worth someone else's manipulation and profit.

Women worldwide are encouraged to aspire to a standard of beauty that has been almost entirely manufactured. What's worse, those images of beauty are created by a system of financial, emotional, and sometimes sexual abuse. So the message that if we are beautiful, we will be happy, famous, successful, sexy, and attract the perfect mate is based on nothing at all. It's a total illusion. But it's a powerful one.

Most women know the pressure of conforming to the images of beauty we are bombarded with every day. For me, too, these images often leave me thinking I need to change my face and my body and fix my big nose and my ugly thighs. Have I contemplated having plastic surgery? Of course I have. I just keep thinking, *Let me see if I can fix my thighs by exercising first* or *Let me save up enough money for the surgery* or *I am too scared right now, but I will get the surgery when I am ready.*

My friend Beth did not have these hesitations. She was beautiful and had always been told she was, starting with her mother, who would compare her to the model Naomi Campbell. She had straight dark hair, flawless skin, and high cheekbones. As an adult, she was a rising star at an elite American publishing firm, with an income that allowed her to work on her image. By the time she reached her early thirties, she had already had a lip augmentation and some injections to prevent wrinkles. In this culture even a naturally beautiful woman is considered perfectible. She also loved fashion. Her clothes were a collection of designer brands, from Jimmy Choo shoes and Dior dresses to Hermès scarves and Chanel purses. Beth was always the first to purchase the latest fashion as soon as a new season arrived. She knew which items were beautiful and fashionable and which ones made the statement she wanted: *successful*.

Whenever she walked into a room, Beth felt admired. She was achieving the beauty she wanted and the life she'd dreamed of.

She was attractive and smart, made good money, and was engaged, with a big diamond ring to show for it. She didn't need to keep working on her looks, but perfecting her image was her obsession. One day she noticed that her left eyelid drooped a little, so she searched through the high fashion magazines, from *Vogue* to *Elle* to *Harper's Bazaar*, for a plastic surgeon who was being featured as the surgeon to the stars.

When she found the right doctor, she didn't hesitate to book the appointment. It was a minor outpatient operation, so she didn't even bother to take much time off work for it. Then her luck turned. During surgery, the surgeon injured a nerve near her eye and left Beth in unbearable pain. She went from specialist to specialist looking for relief. As she searched for a solution, she became dependent on pain medication. She got depressed, gained weight, and started missing a lot of work. She lost her high-power job, along with her fancy friends who had once so admired her beauty and her lifestyle. Her fiancé left her not long after.

Beth's pain imprisoned her, but so did her relationship to beauty. She could not make peace with her new life, so she continued to mimic her old one. She didn't fit into her beautiful clothes anymore, since she was no longer slim. Without her well-paid job, she also could no longer afford the high-end brands. Instead, she bought the fake Dior and the fake Chanel, continuing to search for the labels and the looks that were in season. She could not redefine beauty or find a new identity that was not linked to her appearance. Eventually, she moved away to a new city, looking for a new life with new work and a completely new circle of friends.

Beth is not alone in this pain of not measuring up. I had lived with it, too, as have millions of women and men the world over. When we judge ourselves against the scale of perfection, we will always come up short. Maybe Beth's pain was more intense because she had had that enviable beauty and then lost it. Some of us never even come close. For years, I had a habit of standing in front of my full-length mirror to scrutinize all the things that were not perfect in my face and body. *Not thin enough, not small enough, not big enough, not fit enough, too much this, not enough that*—an onslaught of criticisms would race through my mind. I could see nothing good in my reflection. Listing all my physical faults was a kind of obsessive self-torture. Most every woman I know knows exactly what I'm talking about.

Unlike Beth, I did not grow up thinking I was beautiful. My mother had fed this belief, telling me that my cousin Nadia was much better looking than I was. Whenever she came to visit and we were all invited out somewhere, my mother would insist that I give Nadia my best clothes to wear. At ten years of age, I finally protested: "Why did you give Nadia my orange shirt, Mama? You know it's my favorite."

"But honey," my mother responded. "Nadia is the beautiful one." It was as if beauty itself was reason enough.

My mother didn't think of me as ugly, just not as beautiful as other girls. But the judgment stayed with me. As I grew up, I couldn't see anything pretty or attractive about me. I could see only my prominent, twisted nose and unattractive legs. I took to wearing clothes a size bigger than I needed so that they would hide my imperfections. They ended up hiding all of me.

As I started studying women's rights in college and took on a feminist identity, I also made a statement out of rejecting fashion and beauty. If women around me wore the latest fashionable colors, I wore only black and gray. If they permed their hair or straightened it, I refused to do anything with mine. Rejection became part of my identity, and this continued after college. At important life events, including giving a speech or receiving major awards for my humanitarian work at the White House, I'd wear a simple black and white suit. I wanted to be treated the same as men. I thought that by denying any sense of beauty, I would guarantee that my intellect was noticed, not my looks. I thought this was the higher choice.

But the truth was that whenever I went out with female friends, regardless of their sizes, shapes, and looks, I always felt less beautiful than them. If we entered a restaurant or an event together, I assumed that I was invisible. If we encountered a group of male friends, I never expected any attention from them. I didn't feel jealous; I just felt small.

Still, I kept pushing against that idea that as a woman I needed to be beautiful. I focused on developing my charisma, my personality, my thoughts, and my adventures. I thought it was better for people to love me for my mind. If other women seduced with beauty, I tried to seduce with words and intellect. My unique work in war zones gave me my confidence. But a confident person acts out of fullness, not out of scarcity. I used my activist identity to cover up for my insecurity about my looks. I couldn't appreciate beauty, so I rejected it. That rejection insulted the essence of beauty itself.

It was the women whom I had been helping in war zones who taught me to see beauty in a different way. I was in Sarajevo in 1994, bringing money and clothes to Bosnian women in the besieged city. Their homes—and streets, schools, churches, hospitals, and way of life—were being destroyed by snipers and artillery fire, and they were blockaded inside the city while food and basic supplies dwindled. The only way to enter Sarajevo was on a United Nations plane, and even the UN could not guarantee anyone's safety. I was the only woman in a plane full of French UN troops, crossing Serbian lines to get into the city. At that time, I had heard all about the rape camps and concentration camps in the country. Traveling to Sarajevo was very risky.

With the help of the UN, I made it to the city center without harm, but everywhere the walls were full of shrapnel. People ran from alley to alley to get around, often in a rain of bullets. Everything was scarce—food, water, heat. Many burned their shoes, books, and furniture in the winter for heat. The dead had to be buried in backyards because it was too dangerous to go to cemeteries.

In spite of the danger, I was able to meet with several women's organizations to distribute the funds I had raised for them. It was exciting to meet and hear about their needs and realities and to think about how to help them better. I asked them what else I could bring besides clothes and money. I had in mind vitamins, tampons, bandages, and other practical items.

"Lipstick!" the first woman said. "We want lipstick."

"Lipstick? What?" I was taken aback. Why would they want *lipstick*? They had so many more urgent needs.

"Lipstick is the smallest thing I can put on and feel beautiful," the woman told me. "I want that sniper to know that he is killing a beautiful woman."

Resistance comes in different ways. Some fight back with guns. Some fight back by keeping the music playing, like the Bosnian cellist who played in the middle of an open square where snipers could easily shoot him. Some fight back with art, like the artists who turned empty bullet casings into pieces of art. This woman was fighting back by keeping beauty alive. Putting on lipstick was the simplest way to feel beautiful and connected to life itself. It's how she could triumph over the humiliation of being starved and possibly killed by an unseen gunman.

It suddenly hit me: to deny women their sense of beauty would be to violate their dignity and integrity. Even if they were suffering shortages of food and water, even if they lacked basic hygiene, even if they were cold and afraid, they had every right to ask for cosmetics. These women were not just desperate victims. They wanted to live and die in dignity and to choose their circumstances.

On my following visits to Bosnia, I brought boxes of lipsticks, as well as blush, eye shadow, and all the other makeup I could collect, along with the basics of money, clothes, and food. I also paid attention to how I carried myself and what I wore. I had thought that being a humanitarian activist meant ignoring any sense of beauty, so normally I had just worn my normal jeans and sneakers and pulled my hair back. Once I realized that beauty is part of keeping our spirits alive, I got myself a nice skirt and a matching shirt and a good haircut as well. I wanted to show respect to the women I was working with. They were carrying themselves so elegantly, in spite of the war, in spite of their fatigue. They were coming to meetings in nicely pressed blouses and skirts, even when everything they had—even life itself—was in peril. I wanted to be as presentable as they were trying to be.

Over the years, I have encountered thousands of women in many war zones who carried themselves with this kind of beauty, integrity, and dignity. They would strive for the smallest hint of it even when they were destitute. Behind their head-to-toe burqas, Afghan women wore vibrantly colored clothes—old pieces of silver or patterns of red, orange, and green woven into the belts they had embroidered. Their faces were immaculate—perfect eyebrows, no hair out of place, dark kohl lining their eyes. In DR Congo, women who had been utterly violated and abused danced fiercely and sang with all their hearts whenever they could. It was their way of keeping their spirits alive. If these women who had lost everything could celebrate whatever beauty they had by wearing bright-red lipstick, putting on nice dresses, smiling big smiles, and dancing with their full hearts, then who was I to reject beauty? Who was I to take myself so seriously and not dance, sing, or join in what had kept so many spirits alive?

Beauty is not to be denied, not in myself and not in any other woman or man. It is to be celebrated, encouraged, and protected. It is like hope. When all is lost, when material comfort is gone and loved ones are departed, we can hold onto our spirits by cultivating even small gestures of beauty.

After my experience in Bosnia, I allowed myself to start to explore beauty—what it felt like and what it looked like. I didn't have much money at first, but I experimented with makeup and bought some nice clothes once in a while. Over time, as I earned more, I started buying more. Then I was buying all kinds of makeup and all kinds of clothes, experimenting with looks and materials, getting to know brands, designers, and seasons. Each new purchase brought a rush of excitement, as it did the first two or three times I wore it.

It was a beautiful feeling. It would pick me up when I felt depleted, and it cheered me up when I was blue. I always hunted for bargains, and I shopped the sales from Black Friday to post-Christmas, buying much more than I needed to make sure my money went as far as it could. I bought more and more beautiful clothes, until my closet was overflowing.

Of course, the beautiful feeling I got from making these big purchases did not last. The excitement would fizzle, and I'd be left with a dull feeling of emptiness. The cycle of buying, feeling fulfilled, and landing on empty kept repeating itself. Seeking beauty became a never-ending process of consumption. It was like I was trying to put on a mask of beauty that would dissolve as soon as I brought it to my face.

Throughout this time, I was also not connecting my overconsumption with the people who were making the clothes I was thoughtlessly buying. Yes, I was a women's rights activist, but there was a separation in my mind between my humanitarian work and values and the plights of the unseen workers who were making the clothes. Were they being treated fairly? Making enough money to live on? Or were they being abused, working in dungeons? I never even stopped to think about it.

I was no longer making myself ugly in order to make a statement, but I was also not really addressing the insecurity that underpinned all my purchases. Like so many women, I wanted to feel beautiful, loved, and accepted, and I had bought into the idea that I could buy these feelings. In the process, I was contributing to a system of greed and exploitation. And, ironically, I still did not feel beautiful, no matter how many new clothes or pairs of shoes or pieces of jewelry I bought.

It was a Tibetan woman who finally showed me the true route to my beauty. Yangjin was the daughter of an affluent Tibetan family whose home had been confiscated by Chinese authorities. After they lost everything, her family moved into the hills of Tibet, her father became a sheepherder, and they lived a simple life. She had seen the best and the worst of people as her family went from wealth to poverty, from having servants to being the ones who served. She learned early about the value of life beyond material possessions.

As an adult, Yangjin was determined to preserve and revitalize all aspects of Tibetan culture, from beauty products based on Tibetan recipes to traditional music. When I met her, she was performing a concert in New York along with musicians and singers from around the world. Her voice echoed through the church hall with such a magical force that all of us listening fell into absolute silence. Her sound penetrated our hearts.

A mutual friend connected me to Yangjin just before her concert. She was wearing a red silk robe embroidered with dragons, birds, and flowers that trailed behind her when she walked. Her arms were covered with beaded wooden bracelets, and her neck was wrapped by layers of necklaces. I was in awe. Her style was perfectly contemporary and traditional, artistic yet historic at the same time. She was beautiful and with an amazingly beautiful voice. We became fast friends and would hang out every time she visited the United States.

"One day, you will learn how to see your own beauty and how to care for yourself with love," she told me. I hadn't told her anything about my relationship to beauty, but somehow she knew. "The day you learn how to love yourself, you will see beauty in all parts of yourself."

I had no idea what she was talking about. I felt skeptical, but I nodded anyway. I was infatuated with her and her wisdom. Then she gave me an assignment.

"I want you to meditate on your face every day," she said with authority. "Take a mirror and look into your face with your eyes open. Stay in that meditation for at least ten minutes. Don't miss a day."

Yangjin seemed to know something about self-love, and she definitely knew a lot about meditation, so even though I couldn't understand what she was getting at, I decided to follow her advice.

At home, I went into the bathroom and turned on all the lights around the mirror. How many times had I looked at my face without really seeing it? Every morning and every night, for decades, I would wash my face, brush my teeth, remove makeup or apply creams, and yet I'd only ever seen the spots and blemishes or hair that needed plucking. I had never stood quietly and looked at my face in a non-judgmental way before.

At first, I couldn't meditate on my whole face. There were too many features and too many details. So I decided to focus only on my right eye. But even that single eye had too many details to see all at once. So I decided to focus only on my pupil. I breathed in and out, look-ing and holding the meditation for as long as I could—five minutes, ten, fifteen. Time stretched and contracted as I did the practice. Yet it calmed me. My worries dissolved, and my mind quieted. I didn't have to be anywhere or be anyone.

Then one day something different happened, and it changed every-thing. As I focused on my eye, time suddenly seemed to move at warp speed, and the veil between consciousness and the subconscious lifted. The line between the present moment and eternity dissolved. Space and speechlessness were the same. In an instant, I entered my soul through the door of my eye.

I'd heard the expression "The eyes are the window to the soul" before, but until that moment I had never truly understood it. In that glimpse, I saw beauty, utter beauty, in my soul. It was as beautiful as a flower blooming between the cracks of dry earth, a breathtaking sunrise, a hawk flying through the vast skies. In the soul that lay within me was a pure essence of beauty. I felt nothing but awe for what I was witnessing. It was so beautiful that tears sprang to my eyes.

The meditation left me in a deep, speechless state. As a popular quote attributed to Rumi states, "Silence is the language of God, all else is poor translation." That sacred quality of silence is what I felt. It was like I had seen some beautiful other being inside me who was also a part of me. How could I have not loved it, cherished it, protected it, and nourished it? For all these years I had overlooked it, denied it, rejected it, and even tried to cover it up. How ungrateful I was to have never have paid attention to it!

That day I decided to start showing my appreciation for this inward beauty as it was contained in my physical body. I stood in front of that same mirror in which I had scrutinized my flaws and faults for so many years, and all I could see was beauty. What I had hidden I now celebrated. My gray hairs and my black hairs, my wrinkled skin and my smooth skin were equally beautiful. Every single part of me—every inch, every perfection and imperfection—was God's creation, I realized. Loving it all was part of loving God. Denying it or complaining about it was like being ungrateful to the divine. I touched every part of me from my smallest toes up to the top of my head in gratitude. I thanked my body for its health, for its beauty, for being a part of me. I thanked the thighs that I had always hated as too big, and I thanked the nose that I'd always wished was less prominent. All the parts of me had allowed me to be who I was and function the way I did.

I was forty-four years old; it had been a lifetime of looking and looking for something that had been inside me all along.

Every day since that magical moment in front of the mirror, I have gone over my body in ritual gratitude this way. My relationship to my looks had changed from one of denial to overindulgence to, finally, acceptance and care. I started to give myself all the sleep I needed; I made time to work out and to enjoy the small pleasures of life—the taste of an apple, the sound of a bird, the feeling of sun on the back of my neck. If before I'd felt guilty at giving myself time to play or rest, now I felt a sense of duty to nourish and rejuvenate this body that housed me so well.

As I embraced the beauty inside me, my clothes and my habits began to reflect my values. I found myself buying fewer clothes and shoes, less makeup and less of everything. My beauty and value were no longer so closely attached to what I wore and how I looked, so I no longer binge-shopped at sales. I just didn't feel that same emptiness.

If shopping in the past came out of a need to fill a gap, now shopping came only from a sense of love. Instead of wanting to buy the beautiful shirt in front of me on the rack, I started asking about the story behind it: Who made it? How were they treated? Were they paid well? I began to ask every store about the production policies they supported. I limited my clothes to items that reflected my values: care for the environment and fair labor practices. I'd rather pay for one beautiful, ethically made shirt than for ten shirts that violated the world in some way. I no longer wanted the mask of beauty—I wanted to embody its very essence. In this way, each act became a quest for the essence of what I was buying, whether it was the food I ate, the flowers I bought, or the objects I invested in.

I realize it is not always possible to be fully conscious in each and every purchase. We all have good days and bad days. There are days when I feel heavier, and days when I feel lighter. There are days when I love what I'm wearing, and days when I don't—and days when I don't care one way or the other. There are days when I overindulge in food or I don't buy from an ethical source. But even so, I'm able to come back into equilibrium quickly. I never stop thinking of myself as beautiful, even with my imperfections. I don't automatically lose the connection to my values. Beauty, I now know, helps us to get closer to peace, and peace helps us get closer to God.

I started to give to myself the acceptance that I had wanted from others. I saw there was no better caretaker of this body and soul than me.

When we have intimacy with ourselves, everything inside and outside of us realigns. Our behaviors, attitudes, and choices become anchored in ourselves. For me, this inner freedom is freedom from being told what I should like and how I should be on the basis of someone else's values or standards. I no longer have to follow a commercialized system that tries to bottle the abundance of this world and sell it back to me as scarcity. Beauty emerges from the fullness of a person who knows his or her own goodness and badness, loveliness and ugliness, courage and smallness. Beauty comes from our inner light that knows no color or size or shape. When we see that light in ourselves, we start seeking it in everyone and everything around us. We know it is the essence of beauty, and we no longer need to dominate or manipulate it.

Now, I don't have to compartmentalize my "good" acts apart from my everyday acts. Every day is an act of consciousness, a prayer, and a gratitude for life's gifts: when my feet touch the ground in the morning, when I inhale and exhale, and when my fingers type these words. I no longer need to visit exotic places or buy the latest fashions to feel interesting, valued, and beautiful. I now see and enjoy beauty in the ordinariness of my everyday life. I know that even the smallest stone is part of the largest mountain; just one leaf is part of the fuller forest.

It is not always an easy journey to set your tone in life and live by it. Sometimes, when I don't abide by cultural norms, it feels like I am walking against the wind. But by no longer trying to hide my vulnerabilities, I find deeper and truer connection to others. In these kinds of connections lies a new way of relating to all—to humans, cultures, creatures, and the earth—that is anchored in truth.

When love feels like an endless fountain centered within the self, nothing can replace it. Our soul is our teacher in everything. Until we learn to see it, honor it, and take care of it, we can never know the depth or breadth of our natural beauty. Freedom is an inside job. When we align with it, it can be like the butterfly effect. One small change in our lives, like the air displaced by a butterfly's wing, can have an enormous ripple effect on our entire complex system of interconnected lives. It can change the whole world.

Epilogue

A Call for the New Human Being

The world we live in is a product of our imaginations,
so let's reclaim our imaginations.

We cannot afford to abandon ourselves anymore. Any one of us can become a tyrant when we are blind to our shadows. When we don't center ourselves in our truth and values, our arguments and positions lose credibility, and we risk losing ourselves in a self-declared righteousness. The only way to hold the reins of our lives is to be fully present to the good, the bad, and the ugly that exist in each and every one of us. We show up in our fullness. Then we can stop pointing our fingers at others in fear and anger and start talking and acting from a place of clarity. This is how we avoid destroying ourselves and the world and start building the world we want to live in.

The journey of truth starts with being present to the complexity of our stories, our emotions, and our actions. Our heroes have failed us, so let us not fail ourselves. The true hero is the one whose light and shadow, strength and vulnerability are equally visible. When we are anchored in our full truth and can show compassion for our consistencies and inconsistencies, it becomes easier to hear and see the stories of others from a place of compassion rather than judgment. We can speak knowing our own complexities rather than clinging to an impossible ideal of perfection.

The story of "us" and "them" can be resolved if we all see ourselves in it. Though it is a hard journey and perhaps a never-ending one, it leads to our ultimate freedom. It's where we find how to start a new discussion and a new path forward.

The choice is ours. These days, we are surrounded by fear and division. We can look at these disturbing stories as isolated incidents of foreign terrorists, raving racists, out-of-touch liberals, and corrupt politicians, or we can look at them as part of the fabric of a story that we have all woven together. In the prejudices, fears, and discriminations that we hold in our hearts but have not acknowledged to ourselves, we can become the very things we despise.

If our goal is to find peace, we need to start by acknowledging what is broken. It's a brokenness we've all created together, and it's a brokenness we can all fix together, too. It starts with lowering our walls of fear to hear and see ourselves and one another in a new way.

In the summer of 2017, I visited Mosul, Iraq's second largest city. It was just three weeks after its liberation from the terrorist regime of ISIS (or Daesh, as it's called in Arabic). After three years of extremist rule, the city was completely destroyed. Houses were crumpled into mountains of rebar and concrete. Intersections, bridges, schools, and universities were blown up. Scholarly libraries were burned to ash. Muslim mosques and Christian churches that had honored prophets and saints, legends and scholars were obliterated. It was as if the past fifteen hundred years of faith, thought, and prayer had never happened.

The once sophisticated city of Mosul was decimated, but not its people. As I walked through the streets trying to understand what was needed to rebuild lives and the city itself, I heard people likening what had happened under ISIS to surviving a nuclear bomb. It was the nuclear bomb of human behavior. Some citizens had accepted the self-proclaimed leaders' promises of money, power, and respect, and others had paid little attention, thinking at first that ISIS was just making a power grab that didn't concern them. But the fundamentalists' way of ruling quickly separated people into extreme positions of "us" and "them." Soon, one religious sect was pitted against another, innocent people were hanged in the streets, and daughters and sisters were forced into marriages with ISIS fighters. It became dangerous to even leave the city. ISIS brought a system of extreme oppression and darkness to all.

As I listened to women and men in the streets, in their homes, in recently reopened cafés, restaurants, and workplaces, all of them were saying, "We need a new value system, one that is not based on division, fear, and hatred. We need a new human being."

"We tried religion in its fundamentalist version," said one young man I interviewed in his sisters' home. "We tried to oppress and control women. We tried to say, 'This sect is better than that one' or 'Our religion is better than other religions,' and we failed. That attitude did not work. We destroyed ourselves in the process, and now we are left with nothing."

One man told me if ISIS had ruined the reputation of Islam throughout the world, it had destroyed Islam's role in the lives of Mosul's citizens too.

A woman sweeping her street said, "I will clean the rebel from my house. I will fix the windows and the doors after all this destruction. I can do it myself. I just need help articulating a new value system. This politics of division and blame failed us and destroyed us. We need to start a new way of thinking beyond 'us' and 'them.'"

"We need to start with the children," a policeman said.

Everywhere there was an exciting feeling of unity as citizens began to process what had happened and what was now possible. There was a profound awareness and determination to stop listening to anyone who incited division and hatred. It was as if the people of Mosul had lost themselves, destroyed everything in the process, and woken up with a new commitment to establish new values.

All of us have this choice, not just the people of Mosul. The corruption of our values is not something that just happens to people *over there*. How can we spare *ourselves* from self-destruction, from experiencing the abyss of darkness? How can we wake up to the call for a new human being, one who does not live in fear, blame, anger, and projection? How can we create a new value system—so that we never have to experience the physical and existential destruction that Mosul has?

Soon after visiting Mosul, I returned to New York and attended a gathering of young global leaders at the World Economic Forum. There, too, in this shiny, affluent American city, so different from the rubble of destroyed Mosul, I heard this call for new values. What we are working with is based on systems that are no longer relevant. Division and fear no longer help us. We need this new system not only because of the destruction caused by terrorism and war elsewhere but because of all the division and fear here: in our own nations, in our own families, and in our own hearts.

All of the new technologies and ways of communication that are emerging in our lives—on our phones and in our media and in our collective imaginations—are making it necessary to reexamine our values—for our families, our cities, our villages, our mosques, our churches, our synagogues and temples; in our classrooms and in our relationships; at our conventions and summits. We need a new value system to take us into the future.

I do not claim to know what this new system is. Its articulation can come only from our collective imagination. The world we live in is a product of our imaginations, and together we can reclaim it. I do know that whatever we do or say, we need to start from the very basics, from the foundation, and the foundation is our hearts. When we anchor ourselves in our truth, we can have the courage to live our lives by our hearts' callings and not by the values set for us by constructs outside of us that may be outdated, commercialized, corrupted, or manipulated for someone else's interests and gain.

The journey starts with our stories, but it does not end there. The journey is about finding our truth, acknowledging it, living it, and showing up in a new way in a much-divided world. Together we weave a new story for ourselves, individually and collectively. The taste of freedom is delicious, and it is worth walking the hard journey it may entail to experience it.

Questions for Reflection

CHAPTER 1 Telling Our Stories

- What is the story you are carrying but not sharing?

- Are there secrets you were always told to keep hidden? Is there a part of you that thinks you don't have a story to tell?

- What holds you back from telling your story, no matter how big or small it is? What feelings come up when you imagine breaking your silence?

- Write down your story, even if it's just for yourself. Healing starts with the first articulation of our story.

- Notice how you feel once you've written out your story. Notice all the feelings that come up in the days after this writing.

CHAPTER 2 Living in Truth

- Notice who around you is carrying a story for you. It could be a friend, a family member, a colleague, or a neighbor—anyone you're close to. Think of people who inspire you or those who annoy or upset you.

- What is it about these people that you love or hate, envy or judge? What would happen if you acknowledged these characteristics in yourself? Can you see any evidence of them in your actions, behaviors, or desires already?

- What would life be like if you lived your truth fully? How would it be different than it is today?

- Is any part of you afraid to hurt or disappoint others by living your truth? Do you blame others for your inability to live your truth? Explore this in your imagination.

CHAPTER 3   Owning Our Success

- What attachments to external things such as work or achievements give you a sense of worth? What happens if these attachments are cut off? Who are you then?

- Where in your life have you stopped hearing your truest desires? What used to make your heart beat faster with excitement?

- What stops you from pursuing your truth and dreams? Look fear in the eyes and explore it. What part of it is real, and what part of it is not real? When you stop and get quiet, your heart will let you know.

- You will be tested if you take a leap of faith. Do you have a support system around you to hold you and remind you that you are not alone?

CHAPTER 4   Making Amends

- What story of shame are you carrying but not talking about? What story have you not been willing to admit?

- Why are you afraid to confront your story of shame? What do you have to lose if you try to make amends? When we don't face our fears and get ahead of them, they are more likely to come true.

- Start taking the first step in telling your story of shame. Acknowledge it however you want: by writing it down, by telling it to a trusted friend or in a safe group, or by working with an expert, such as a counselor or psychologist.

- What did you learn about yourself and about the world from acknowledging your story of shame?

- When you are ready, make amends with the person or people you need to. It will be your biggest gift to them and to yourself. By acknowledging their story, you will be lifting their burden and pain, and that will ease your own guilt and shame.

CHAPTER 5   Going Into Our Darkness

- How have you hurt people in your life? What part of your personality inflicts this hurt? Can you look at this part of yourself directly, without giving excuses or justifications for what you do?

- What do you dislike the most in people's characters? What does such dislike trigger in you?

- What if instead of pointing the finger at what you don't like in others, you pointed the finger at yourself? What might you see if you did that?

- What would it take to transform your own shadow? Not destroy it, but transform it. What are the incentives to change?

- Can you show compassion to your own shadow? Can you use it to ignite certain positive actions and not get stuck or entrenched in it?

CHAPTER 6   Forgiving Ourselves First

- Notice when you dismiss your gut feeling about another person's actions. What motivates you to dismiss your instincts? What part of you is betraying you?

- We all have our insecurities, fears, and worries. What part of you is scared? What does it want? Go to this place in yourself and try to understand it honestly. What is it all about? When you see it, hold it and love it. It can show you the way toward true forgiveness of yourself.

- Look at those who have hurt you the most in your life. Try to see the insecure part of them as you have seen the insecure part of yourself. In their pain, they have caused pain. Seeing this is the first step toward forgiving them.

- Bring to mind those you have hurt the most in your life. Owning your part of the story is humbling, but it is also interesting to be in the humble seat. It requires courage and authenticity. Imagine sitting before them, asking for forgiveness. Do it, not because they are asking you to, but so you can clear the noise in your own head. It will also allow you to show compassion toward others when the roles are reversed.

CHAPTER 7   Surrendering Control

- What do you really want to happen in your life that is not happening the way you want it to?

- In your definition, have you showed up in all the ways you can to make your ambitions or dreams come true? Have you not just made your intention but also acquired the necessary skills and experience?

- No matter how you answered the questions above, take a step back to breathe. Don't make any effort to fulfill your goals for a while. Instead, be present in the moment.

- You may notice restlessness or anxiousness in yourself for "not doing" anything, but just "being." Hold that feeling and observe it rather than doing what you usually do.

- Notice what comes up—a thought, some words, something you recall about yourself or someone else.

- Open your eyes and notice all the ordinary beauty around you, things you may be overlooking in your focus to get what you want. What do you see?

CHAPTER 8 Freedom Is an Inside Job

- What do you not like about your looks? What do you like?

- Whom would you most like to resemble?

- What shortcuts are you taking to get where you want to go? Are these harming you or others?

- Where are you disconnected in your eating habits, in your shopping, or in your relationship to your body? How can you work on creating a connection instead?

- Meditate on your face. Find one spot you can focus on and keep your gaze there for five to ten minutes. Let go of any expectations. Do this every day and see what arises. You may see an abundance of beauty you never knew you had all along.

Acknowledgments

Thanks to all those who have helped in making this book possible. It starts with Caroline Pincus, for her wonderful support and guidance in finding this book a home at Sounds True. Gratitude to Joelle Hann, my editor and partner in crime in the writing process, for her questions, patience, and support as I worked on articulating my thoughts and for all her hard work in turning the book into its final version. Special thanks to Jane Isay for helping me focus the book in its early phase of development. The friendship that came out of that is a most beautiful gift. Finally, thanks to my agent, George Greenfield, who has had my back for many years.

Everything shared in this book came from experiences that taught me about love in all its forms—from the deep love and support of my family and friends, to passing but meaningful connections with strangers, and even to conflicts with foes who have hurt me. Throughout all these experiences, I came to learn that love is bigger than all and is above all.

Out of respect for everyone's privacy, I have changed most people's first names in the book. But there are those whose names must be mentioned here, for they have impacted the learning journey of my life. My father, Tariq Salbi, and my two brothers and their families are the joy of my life. I am forever grateful to have been born to a family in which love was always its foundation. My dearest friends, Maureen Chiquet, Vuslat Dogan Sabanci, and Peggy Dulany, anchor my life with their wisdom, insight, love, and joy. Deepest gratitude to Barry Williams and A. B. for guiding me in my darkest hours and to my friend Patricia Gruber, who believed in and supported me even when I thought I had failed.

The teachings of my dear friend Alice Walker and my late mentor Angeles Arrien are woven throughout the book. I offer heartfelt thanks to Virginia McKenzie, who has so generously shared the wisdom and traditions of her people, the Anishinabe Nation, with me over the years. Amjad Atallah, my former husband, is my teacher in love before marriage, during marriage, and after marriage. I am grateful to him and to his wonderful wife, Stephanie Bagot, for welcoming me into their family.

Thanks to Michael Peterson for his friendship and support from near and afar. And thanks to Ali Sabanci and the late Reda Gargour, whose friendships provided so much safety, love, and care. Warmest thanks to Jochen Zeitz for being so inspiring in his actions to change the world for the better through his conservation work at Segera Retreat, which provided me much learnings from all the animals and earth's wisdom.

Warm gratitude to my friend Donna Karan, who helped me own my beauty and see the artist within; to Dr. Charles Passler, who helped me relate to food and my body in new ways; and to my friends Begum Dogan Faralyali, Basma Alireza, Kathy Karn, Renata Williams, Tess Beasley, and Barry Walker for indulging my processing of the different moments of my life with so much loving patience and care. Special thanks to Tina Brown for all her support and trust; to Swanee Hunt for all the stories, tears, and laughter that we shared in the fight for women's rights and our climb of Kilimanjaro; to Ahmer Kalam for his amazing creative work and friendship; and to Katy Davis, Suzanne Haywards, and Alpay Guler for their guidance, hard work, and support of my media projects.

Gratitude to Monica Winsor, Barry Segal, Mercedes Zobel, and Dounia Benjelloun for their loving support; to John Botts for his belief in me when I felt I was alone and for his support and guidance in the journey of making my dreams a reality; and to my friends Neal Goldman and Javier Macaya for their solid friendships and most honest conversations.

My utmost gratitude goes to Oprah Winfrey. She is an angel in this world and an angel in my life who has supported me directly and indirectly over the years. I am grateful to her for featuring the work of

Women for Women International several times on *The Oprah Winfrey Show*, exposure that raised tremendous support for women survivors of war. I am also grateful to her for giving me her first interview to the Muslim and Arab world through the Arabic show I launched, *The Nida'a Show*. Meeting her led to life-changing conversations that helped me to own my voice in profound ways.

Last but not least, thanks to all the women I have had the honor of meeting through my work in conflict areas. Each smile, each word, each face is forever imprinted in my heart. These women have been my ultimate teachers in love and in the goodness of humanity.

About the Author

Zainab Salbi has frequently been named one of the women changing the world by leading publications ranging from *Newsweek* to *People* magazine. Most recently, *Foreign Policy* magazine named her one of "100 Leading Global Thinkers."

At the age of twenty-three, Zainab founded Women for Women International, a humanitarian organization dedicated to women survivors of wars. Under her leadership (1993–2011), Women for Women International grew from helping 30 women upon its inception to helping more than 420,000 women and distributing more than one hundred million dollars in aid.

Zainab is the author of several books, including the bestseller *Between Two Worlds: Escape from Tyranny: Growing Up in the Shadow of Saddam* (with Laurie Becklund); *The Other Side of War: Women's Stories of Survival and Hope*; and *If You Knew Me You Would Care* (with photographs by Rennio Maifredi).

She is also the executive editor and host of the *#MeToo, Now What?* series on PBS, *The Zainab Salbi Project* with Huffington Post and AOL, and *The Nida'a Show* with TLC Arabia. She is currently the editor at large at Women in the World.

About Sounds True

Sounds True is a multimedia publisher whose mission is to inspire and support personal transformation and spiritual awakening. Founded in 1985 and located in Boulder, Colorado, we work with many of the leading spiritual teachers, thinkers, healers, and visionary artists of our time. We strive with every title to preserve the essential "living wisdom" of the author or artist. It is our goal to create products that not only provide information to a reader or listener, but that also embody the quality of a wisdom transmission.

For those seeking genuine transformation, Sounds True is your trusted partner. At SoundsTrue.com you will find a wealth of free resources to support your journey, including exclusive weekly audio interviews, free downloads, interactive learning tools, and other special savings on all our titles.

To learn more, please visit SoundsTrue.com/freegifts or call us toll-free at 800.333.9185.

SOUNDS TRUE
many voices, one journey